CIA 101

A Crash Course in Agency Case Officers

Professor Millick

185 Sheets
8.5 x 5.5 in / 21.59 x 13.97 cm

CIA 101: A Crash Course in Agency Case Officers

Cover Design and Interior Layout by Melissa Williams Design

Contents

Introduction

Lesson One

The Meaning of Life 10

Lesson Two

No Superheroes 22

Lesson Three

A Secular God 29

Lesson Four

Make-Believe 39

Lesson Five

Purgatory 53

Lesson Six

PCS 62

Lesson Seven

What Would You Say You Do Here? 77

Lesson Eight

C/Os as Agents 99

Lesson Nine

What Do Spies and Lovers Have in Common? 109

Lesson Ten

A Closed System 116

Lesson Eleven

Why the Good Ones Leave 123

Lesson Twelve

Why the Bad Ones Stay 135

Lesson Thirteen

The CIA at War 147

Lesson Fourteen

The Agency Makes You a Nihilist 171

Acknowledgments

About the Author

He who has a why to live for can bear almost any how.

—Friedrich Nietzche

The great artist is he who conquers the romantic in himself.

—Henry Miller

What destroys the dream? What destroys it, eh? . . .
Disappointment. Disappointment . . . Disappointment.

—Anthony Burgess

Introduction

As a kid, I dreamed of being a communist dictator. I wanted to rule my own country, compel others to salute and sing songs in my honor. But as luck would have it, I was born too late for that to be a realistic option.

When I got older, I wanted a job that was just as exciting. What were some other possibilities? Mob boss, movie star . . . international explorer.

And spy. A hero who lives and works in exotic foreign countries, conducts espionage, and sews intrigue at the highest levels of power.

The Central Intelligence Agency—specifically, the Directorate of Operations, or DO—actually hires for that position, the "second-oldest profession," as the saying goes. They pay a regular salary. And I wouldn't have to become a mob boss, which made my parents happy.

Case Officer, C/O for short, is the official job title—not to be confused with caseworker, which is what my Mom first assumed. And like a good mom, she immediately told her sister about my super-secret application.

As a side note, you can quickly tell the authenticity of a spy book or movie by how it refers to the profession. For example, if it calls a C/O an "intelligence agent," the writer has little credibility on the subject. Agents are the human sources hired by Case Officers, also referred to as "assets." And if someone calls a C/O an "operator" or "operative," they're just trying to sound Hollywood.

Others mix up the meanings of covert and clandestine, but who can blame them? Covert sounds so much cooler.

While we're on the topic, no one in the biz calls the CIA "the Company"—except as a joke. It's simply the Agency. If you want to sound old-school, you might say "the Outfit." Other old-schoolers, especially senior-level types, leave off "the," calling it merely "CIA."

Also, no one refers to Agency headquarters in Northern Virginia as "Langley"—that's more Hollywood nonsense. CIA HQS is simply called, well, "HQS."

So if you want to "spot the spooks" in the theatre while watching a Hollywood spy movie, scan for the ones laughing during the serious scenes.

The thing is, C/Os are not really spies. They recruit and handle spies—the ones who commit treason, betray their countries, and will be punished severely if things go wrong. Spies will be imprisoned, shot, or hanged. But C/Os don't usually take much risk and, when something bad happens, they'll probably end up with a slap on one hand and a "Get-Out-of-Jail-Free" card in the other.

Don't get me wrong. C/Os like to refer themselves in equally romantic terms. When managers feel rambunctious, they remind the workforce that, despite all the political correctness these days, they work at a spy agency, which means their job is to lie, cheat, and steal—and more specifically, to steal secrets.

It all sounds so badass, like C/Os are a bunch of ninjas creeping around a secret government facility. God bless Hollywood. They've helped C/Os impress the ladies for decades.

But in reality, while your average Case Officer does quite a bit of lying and cheating—though not always at work or for the benefit of the mission—he's less active in the stealing department. In fact, he may collect secrets, but he rarely takes them—or anything else, for that matter.

The truth is, only on rare occasions does the Agency actually break into homes and offices to grab information. This type of work is done by non-C/Os—those highly trained in disguises, lock picking, and physical construction, or deconstruction, in this case.

C/Os pay others to steal things for them, like those agents mentioned above. And even then, "steal" is a misnomer. Most agents on the books don't do much actual thieving. They simply tell their handler what they know, the scoop about their government jobs, and what they overheard from fellow criminals and terrorists.

Looked at pedantically, how do you swipe an idea or a piece of information? To take something implies a physicality to it and a chance that you won't get it back. But like gossip, secrets largely exist in the air. They are intangible, impermanent, and often hard to trace—which is why they're so often wrong. They can be overheard and repeated, even copied, which proves they're not exactly one-of-a-kind items.

That's not to say that human intelligence isn't worthwhile. It is. Some of it is. A little bit, maybe. But much of it is worthless. It's been said before, and I'll say it here again: so much of what's collected is never even read, let alone digested, or—can I get a hallelujah?—actually used in foreign policy decisions. Most of it is simply stored in a giant, Indiana-Jonesy virtual warehouse. Collection has become both an endless means and a meaningless end.

As for me, I learned these realities too late, after I was already hooked on joining the CIA. And when my sights are set, I'm a veritable dog with a chew toy—it takes a lot to convince me to let it go.

But I digress.

I swore when I joined the CIA that I would never write a kiss-and-tell book. You know the books I'm talking about. The chest-thumping, "There I was on the streets of Paris or Pyongyang" tell-alls that are shockingly permitted to give away the keys to the kingdom, largely to inflate otherwise tiny egos and make the authors seem like real-life superheroes. You can practically smell the hubris in their pages.

If I *were* to write such an account, I'd say things like: I completed six tours, spent twenty years overseas, served in a dozen different countries, visited fifty more, and worked in every major war zone. I recruited agents in strange lands, late at night, on dark, dusty roads. I handled terrorists and criminals and foreign officials in high-threat scenarios. I went after Taliban and al-Qa'ida fighters on their home fields in Africa and South Asia, contributed to their eliminations and arrests, and interrogated them in prison after capture. I was shot at by all kinds of weapons. I jumped out of airplanes. I carried a pistol stuck in my pants and a rifle on my back. I raced cars and smashed through barricades. I shot nearly every type of rifle and machine gun. I threw grenades and Molotov cocktails and worked with plastic explosives.

In short, my life could be made into a movie, played by one of those so-called Hollywood stars whose own life never goes beyond the pretend world.

But as I said—I would never do that.

Not just for the sake of discretion. In part, it's because such a book, if told truthfully, would end up much shorter than this one. You see, vast amounts of a

C/O's career are just not that exciting—spoiler alert for the real reason officers don't usually write such a book—that, and because most of them don't write very well. Sure, there are some thrilling, heart-pounding moments that virtually no one else will share, moments which make you eternally grateful for choosing this path, especially when you overhear non-Agency friends swapping mind-numbing water cooler stories at the neighborhood barbecue.

But these are few and far between, more like valuable bookends on a long shelf packed with endless staff meetings and answering dumb questions from a HQS desk officer, rather than parachute jumps into enemy territory and passing money to a coup leader.

To some, the purpose of a kiss-and-tell book is to euphemistically "set the record straight." In practice, we know this actually means to get revenge and badmouth some person or group in order to make yourself look and feel better. When you write such a book, you are, in effect, redefining your loyalty by proclaiming to the world why you don't believe in this or that anymore.

But I still have faith in the Agency. I want its C/Os to be the best in the business. And unlike many today, I believe in the utter necessity of having a powerful spy agency—yes, even in a democracy.

The CIA gave me everything. It provided extraordinary training and momentous experiences. It granted me a chance to serve my country, to meet unique people and playmakers around the world, to not only see but take part in history. It allowed me to do things others only dream about. In short, the Agency gave me a monumental life.

To me, the CIA, its history and heritage, its founders and traditions, its ongoing mission, are essentially sacred.

But the people? That's another matter—especially these days.

If you want an ultra-short description of this crash course, it would read something like: The CIA: great place, kind of lousy people. Or: The CIA: fascinating and unique career, sub-par professionals.

Now for a longer description. This book is a bunch of Jackson Pollack-type splotches thrown at a canvas. It's a collection of impressions in essay-form about a little-known place and a few of its employees, written by someone who worked there for twenty years. The book is an intimate look at Case Officers—what they do and what they're like—and what it's really like to work at the Agency. It's a peek behind the curtain—at least, as much as the censors will allow—that includes both what you need to know and what's *neat* to know.

So fair warning. This is not a standard *me*-moir about the CIA bound to catch your eye in a bookstore. There will be few tales of James Bond-like derring-do, and none that could expose the Agency's operations. Nor will you hear me badmouth the organization or its reasons for being. Simply put, I have nothing to avenge. I would rather write a love letter to that semi-mythical place, but it would end up far too mushy.

In fact, my hope is that you'll learn very little about me in this book. Like a good C/O, I don't crave the limelight or feel comfortable talking about myself. I was taught instead to let my background and experience speak for themselves. I'm grateful to the Agency for recognizing my good points without forcing me to self-promote.

So why did I write this book? To have a little fun,

to laugh at silly events and a sometimes kooky career, to expose the profession through a lens of honesty and humor, rather than Hollywood melodrama. Perhaps, after endless CIA evaluations, I want to turn the tables for a change.

Most of all, I'd like to help attract better officers to the field by establishing some expectation management about the place, the job, and the other employees—so the good ones won't run away when harsh reality inevitably collides with outrageous expectations. The Agency itself has declared the search for truth to be paramount. I want to inspire applicants to want this job for the right reasons.

Since I've already left, I tried to write the book as an objective, third-person observer who was just passing through. I admire anthropologists who visit strange, exotic cultures and report back on what the people are like in a detached, unemotional way. And for the most part, that's what I tried to do: describe the Agency, how it works—and how it doesn't—in a way that does no harm to the natives but may help educate the next generation that will join them in the future. And maybe, my words will spark some small change in how the place is run, how new officers are hired, and what eventually happens to those officers.

Despite my interest in anthropology, I was a history major. And as a good historian, analysis, especially when it comes to human behavior, runs in my blood. I can't examine an event and *not* try to explain why people made certain decisions.

This applies to social situations as well. Like George Costanza, I can sense immediately when a person feels uncomfortable, even when his life's out of balance. Give me a few minutes with him, and I can tell you why—making me a bit of a "human whisperer," if you will. This tendency, as explained later, is employed by good C/Os every day.

What's my secret? I don't have super strength. But I was born with an inordinately high level of empathy. For some reason, I can put myself in other peoples' shoes and understand them pretty easily. That is my only superpower.

Some may find the tone of the book irreverent—especially those officers with high opinions of themselves. Perhaps unintentionally, one lesson I learned in my career was that much of life is silly (even absurd, if you're a French intellectual) and should be laughed at, rather than brooded over. As a result, the narrative can take a sarcastic and sassy tone. By the end, you may see why my mouth has gotten me into trouble since I was five years old.

Others may see the book as dystopian, as if nothing ever goes right in the world of espionage. That's not the case. Lots of things go right—or at least don't fall apart. But just as a book of high-stakes exploits would be too short, a collection of normal, quiet days would be too long and surely not worth their space in ink. If anything, my attempt is simply a realistic, rather than idealistic, view of the organization with a descriptive, rather than judgmental, bend.

When I reflect on my career, I often find myself laughing or shaking my head, not squinting like Clint Eastwood or the protagonist in a Hollywood chest-thumper. This sentiment is what made it on to the page.

Because in the end, if it's not fun, it's probably not worth doing, at least not for long—which is one of the reasons why I (and many others) don't work there anymore.

Of course, there are serious aspects to the Agency. I haven't turned into a complete nihilist. I'll end on one of those notes. Despite the book's sarcasm, I hope you see the good that the CIA does. That you have reason to be proud of those officers who work hard and risk their lives for the good of their country. That you hope more good people will enter its doors.

So there you have it. I didn't write a kiss-and-tell, after all.

Lesson One

The Meaning of Life

"Action and adventure"—that's my impetuous answer when asked why I joined the CIA. Because what else is there in life?

But I could add: I wanted a career with some kind of meaning, a higher purpose, even. A career where I could serve the country and put my stamp on the world.

Now, digging a little deeper, my decision to join was triggered by both a push and a pull.

The push came from the need to escape a country past its prime, with glory days fading in the rearview window. And to escape a people who wanted very different things than me, who valued little more than safety and comfort. In short, my American Dream was to flee America.

(You are correct to note the irony of someone who wanted to serve a country he couldn't stand living in—a common conundrum of many expatriates.)

The pull, naturally, came from the opposite direction, driven by a ferocious desire to see the big, beautiful world. I wanted to find those who lived differently, who hadn't been corrupted by things like common sense. I wanted to know those who were interested in the more intangible sides of life.

In the process, I hoped to follow in the footsteps of

heroes like Hemingway and Thoreau, who left home to test their own mettle, challenge their deep-set fears, and learn about themselves. Afterwards, both reflected upon and wrote about their experiences.

I believe strongly in Fate, that there is a path you're supposed to take. I also believe the right path is often the hardest, which is why so many try to avoid it.

Another way of putting it is, God wants you to have a lot in life. But He won't just give it away—proving you deserve it is up to you. So how badly do you want it? In my experience, the answer to that question usually determines success or failure.

It's like qualifying for the next level of your favorite video game, gradually moving up, one step at a time. Sure, you're welcome to remain at "Level One" your entire life—but you won't see much of that big, beautiful world.

After all, life is short and precious. You might as well grab as many experiences as possible, because there's plenty of time to sleep later in life and not enough of it while you're young.

For me, these tests needed to take place overseas. I wanted to leave everything behind, to become an expatriate. That was the life for me.

But how do you get there? Who will pay you to see the world?

You could join the Army, become a missionary or a diplomat. Or sign up as a spy—I mean, a C/O.

No matter which path you choose, you will have the chance to be a modern-day explorer.

But how do you join the CIA? Is it even a realistic option? After all, the Agency receives thousands and thousands of applications every year for relatively few positions.

I guess that's about right, though. For the C/O position is, as they themselves say, "The Ultimate International Career." Again—what else is there in life?

Clearly, the odds are against you, as they were for me.

I first interviewed at the CIA right out of college. I had graduated with a degree in medieval history and was ready to take on the world. Little did I know that the Agency receives so many applications, that I had virtually nothing to offer other than a high GPA and a sincere wanderlust.

It was the early nineteen-nineties. I interviewed at an office building in Northern Virginia, where the recruiter said flatly that I had a good college record but not enough life experiences. "Go out into the world, experience life, and try again," he said.

So I did.

I attended graduate school at an ancient university in England, following my passion for history. This was probably the only time in my life when my expectations were actually exceeded by the experience.

I fell so hard for the place, I nearly sidestepped my previous ambition. I considered staying on for a PhD and becoming a history professor. Ultimately, I came to a crossroads and had to decide whether to remain in academia or rejoin the real world.

I loved history. But did I really want to live vicariously, spending my career reading about others who had done great things in the past?

Or did I want to witness the people and events of future history books in person, on the front lines, in the present day? To see history while it was happening and maybe play an actual role in it?

Thankfully, I rediscovered my personal "Meaning of Life," rekindling my desire to join the Agency—a final decision corroborated by my observations of fellow classmates who also planned to conquer the world.

After graduation, I stayed overseas, moving this time to the Balkans. For two years, I taught, researched, and explored post-communist southeastern Europe, thereby learning even more about the world and myself.

I moved back to the US in the summer of 1996, pockets stuffed full of credentials. I was ready to reapply to the CIA.

This may sound arrogant, but at this point, I had become an ideal candidate for the Case Officer position. I will temper this apparent bravado by admitting I wasn't really qualified to do much else in life. But in addition to a strong resume, I had other, more intangible, traits that equipped me for this line of work.

First, I had spent my entire life moving, literally and figuratively, between social groups, economic classes, US states, and foreign countries.

My family relocated a half dozen times before I even left for college—in essence, I'd been on the move since I was six months old. It is a sudden, dramatic education and maturation process for a kid to repeatedly start new schools, essentially on his own, and quickly make friends. I was forced to reach out to others, to become interesting and affable, no matter how much it cost me. In that process, I learned social skills and techniques that bordered on survival, but served me well later in life.

I also failed on many occasions. Of course, I did. But to paraphrase Garrison Keillor, rejection has acted as the engine on my back, driving me to go out and do great things. It may also explain why I was obsessed with joining a special, mostly closed organization that few will ever see.

To help my brother and me adjust to our new surroundings, my parents threw us into every sport imaginable—from baseball, football, and basketball, to golf and gymnastics, tennis, racquetball, and downhill skiing. In England, I tried my hand at cricket and rugby and rowed crew.

As an adult, I moved overseas on my own. There, I had to thrive not only among new faces, but strange cultures and unfamiliar languages.

I made it a point to travel between social and economic groups. On one level, I studied at a legendary English university and was tutored by the best in the field. I hobnobbed with the upper crust in medieval colleges, met royals and richies at polo matches, even dated the daughter of a Russian billionaire oligarch.

But in my free time, I hitchhiked Eastern Europe, rode in trucks and horse carts, slept in fields and train stations. Back home in the States, I attended a Grateful Dead show one day, a Slayer concert the next, and finished off the weekend with a ballet.

In short, I learned to blend in among any level of society, moving between worlds easily—from bums to bourgeoisie, peasants to prime ministers, hippies, headbangers, and snobs, I can relate to just about anyone, even without a strong attachment to any of them.

Perhaps the best result of this transient life is that it has allowed my natural curiosity to thrive. Even to this day, I am perpetually interested in what goes on around me.

Mining the depths of intangibility even further, I had another trait that made me a good Case Officer: I was often the last person suspected of doing, well, anything. Despite my successes, I rarely promoted myself, leading others to think of me as relatively safe, mainstream, a minimal threat. I just wasn't often considered by my peers. This kept me off that radar and allowed me to get what I want, both before and after I joined the Agency.

In the end, I was the one who quietly got the prettiest girl, attended elite schools, won the coolest job. Indeed, such success seems counterintuitive in our loud, fake-it-till-you-make-it culture. But I am living proof that it still pays to be the quiet man.

My ability to glide between social classes was an important trait for the Agency—still is, since you never know who you might meet. Targets range from peasant warlords to suburban extremists to Oxford-educated government ministers.

So even though my dream job was still a long shot, the stars finally seemed aligned. I proudly mailed a fresh copy of my resume and waited. Two weeks later, a CIA recruiter telephoned me.

The conversation was so pleasant and easy, it felt like a chat with an old friend. She asked some questions about my background and education and scheduled a personal interview for a few weeks later.

In the meantime, the CIA sent a packet with background information on Case Officers, including a list of memoirs written by former personnel, in the hopes of giving applicants an idea of what to expect. Perhaps foolishly, I didn't read a single book. I wasn't in this to peek behind the curtain and listen to others' experiences.

I'd done plenty of that as a history student. This time, I wanted my own adventure.

So in the fall of 1996, five years after my first failed interview, I stepped into another Agency building in Northern Virginia to try again.

The day began with a group presentation. There were several dozen of us, all well-dressed, all eager to join a legendary organization. A seasoned Case Officer provided an overview of his profession, laced with a few sanitized war stories to get our juices flowing. If we were still interested in the job, he said, they would schedule our personal interviews.

I was still interested in the job.

I returned to the same building a few days later for a ninety-minute interview. Fortunately, I hit it off again, this time with a female C/O behind the desk, and the discussion flowed just as naturally as had the phone interview.

She didn't ask boring, cliché questions, such as "why do you want this job?" Or "what would you bring to the Agency?"

Instead, she got straight to the meaty part, providing instructions, like "give an example of when you manipulated a person or situation to get what you wanted." Fortunately, I'd had a recent experience that hit that mark.

I'd been on a flight to the Balkans and had brought a dog on board. Despite being assured by the airline that the tiny crate would fit under the economy class seat, it didn't—and I really didn't want to check her into the baggage compartment. I explained the situation to a stewardess, all the while showing off an adorable golden retriever puppy to garner her sympathy. She returned a few minutes later to guide us to a roomier seat, under which the dog's box fit easily. Though relatively insignificant, I had leveraged the stewardess's feelings while breaking the rules in order to get what I wanted. And Josie and I enjoyed a free upgrade to business class.

At the earlier presentation, the C/O advised that we would receive a lengthy security questionnaire to fill out if we passed the first step. At the end of the interview, she handed me that packet. Huzzah! I'd made it to the next level.

When the C/O mentioned that the forms were lengthy, he wasn't kidding. It took days to complete a barrage of questions that covered major events in my life for the past ten to fifteen years. I described where I'd lived, worked, attended school. Finally, I scribbled my signature and mailed the papers back to the Agency.

And waited.

About a month later, I received a letter inviting me back to Northern Virginia for more in-depth tests and interviews. Little did I know then, this phase was referred to on the inside as "Hell Week."

Now, five days of personal interviews, psych tests, more interviews, medical tests, polygraph—twice, IQ and writing tests are definitely not fun. But I wouldn't call them "hell," necessarily. Thorough, perhaps, and mildly annoying. But what did I expect?

Five of us endured the week together: a lawyer from New Hampshire, a Navy SEAL from San Diego, a businessman from Florida, a generalist who had lived for a few years in England, and me.

We moved from office to office, completing interviews, listening to briefings about the Agency, learning about the application process. In the evenings, we ate dinner together, complained, and compared notes. As far as I know, only the lawyer and I eventually made it.

Pretty sure the guy from Florida did not.

After our polygraph tests on the second day, he and I sat at the hotel bar, moaning about the painful experience, when out of the blue, two unusually friendly women began chatting us up. The Florida applicant almost immediately gave us up—bragging that we were in town to interview for sensitive government jobs, jobs that required polygraphs that we'd taken earlier in the day. The women couldn't keep their eyes off him.

My stomach sank. I elbowed him and whispered, "I don't think we're supposed to say things like that." And although I'll never know for sure, I still assume the women were security officers sent to see how much we would disclose to random strangers.

The psychological evaluation was the most interesting for me. During the interview, a shrink asked me to describe myself in three words, a thought-provoking experiment for anyone. My mind raced: What does he want to hear? Should I be honest? And to this day, I still remember what I went with: "Smart, sociable, and goal-oriented." While accurate, I figured my response also covered the most important bases for the position.

The written test had several hundred statements to which you answered merely "sometimes," "always," or "never," depending on how you felt about them. Some statements were repeated, likely to see if you recorded the same (true) answer or had merely written what you thought the examiner wanted to hear. Perhaps that was another purpose of the test—to see if you were consistently honest.

The statements covered expected topics—childhood,

lifestyle, social preferences—but three stuck with me: "I'm terrified of windstorms"; "I prefer baths to showers"; and "I will cross the street to avoid meeting someone I don't like." I still have no idea what the *right* answers were, but I would love to meet—and have a beer with—the psychologist who came up with that test.

There were two separate personal job interviews, again with experienced Case Officers. For me, these went well, and I clicked with both female interviewers. This wasn't particularly surprising—not because I'm much of a ladies' man, but because strong women have played significant roles throughout my life—from my Mom, to my college professors, to my wife, to these four Agency officers.

They posed questions that contained operational role-playing, such as: "You're meeting with an agent in your car late at night in a Middle Eastern country. Suddenly, the agent has a heart attack and needs medical attention. What do you do?"

I provided some kind of reasonable answer, like: "First, I'd make sure he didn't have any compromising material on him. Then, I'd drop him off in front of a hospital and get out of the area as quickly as possible. If questioned, I'd respond that the stranger flagged me down for help on the side of the road."

Years later, recruiters revealed scarier answers they'd received from the same question. One applicant responded that he would put a bullet in the agent's head. The interviewer repeated the answer back to him to make sure she understood. "Yes, that's right," he confirmed. "Better for him to die in the car than be exposed as a spy."

There were other strange moments during the week.

Some were probably related to signing a waiver on the first day that allowed the Agency "to monitor and surveil" interviewees during that period of time. For example, someone knocked on my hotel room at about 11pm every night, but by the time I went to the door, there was no one there.

The Navy SEAL applicant was also suspicious to me. I felt he may have been an Agency officer planted in the group to surveil us outside the office. First, he took none of the briefings seriously, acting as though he'd heard them a thousand times. He also told me he grew up in the town where I attended college but was oddly reluctant to say much about the place. Hmm.

On the last day, he and I had completed our final written tests and sat side-by-side in the personnel office. I felt awkward about leaving the building without a final good-bye. Navy SEAL said, "You want to say goodbye to them, to have that closure, don't you?" as if taking notes on me in his head.

I did. But it was over, and there were no such goodbyes.

The end of Hell Week and my part in the application process were complete, with nothing more to do but wait. This had been my life for three months, my dream for years. But I was told it could take another six to twelve months before they made a final decision.

So I waited. And walked the dog. The CIA was my endgame—the only place I had applied. If I weren't accepted, I'd return to Europe and teach, then try again in another few years. I didn't want any other job.

Then, in the spring of 1997, after months of silence and agony, the phone rang in the middle of the afternoon. It is still the biggest and best call of my life.

"Elizabeth" had some very good news, she said. "They" (she never mentioned the Agency) were pleased to offer me a GS-9/6 position in the next training class, starting in about three months. I admit, as much as I wanted to sound professional, I think I just babbled. That's how excited I was.

And just like that, I was a CIA Case Officer. I'd survived all the oral and written tests, the investigations, the poking and prodding by doctors and nurses, examinations by psychologists, evaluations by experienced personnel.

I'd made it.

The only one happier than me was my Mom. I'd finally achieved her hopes and dreams—her son had landed a respectable job that paid a good salary. What else could she want?

She immediately took me shopping for respectable clothes. After all, I owned nothing nicer than khakis and beat up loafers. She also bought me a standard-issue, beige raincoat to, you know, look the part.

I was dying to start work and meet my fellow classmates. We had beaten out an enormous number of applicants for the position, so we had to be a special group.

We had to be.

Lesson Two

No Superheroes

We Americans love superheroes. Don't believe me? Just check out the lineup at your local movie theatre. We'd all love a few real superheroes, I suppose, to help us out now and then.

But Americans also value equality and a level playing field. Let's be real—we don't actually want others to have more power than we do, but we are willing to make exceptions when they use that power for good.

There are also temporal jobs upon which we bestow superhero status. CIA Case Officer is one of them. Others include Navy SEAL and FBI Agent, and movies only back up this mythology.

Few people know what a C/O really does, due to the secrecy of the work. Yet it's revealing to see how imagination fills that void. Most carry around images in their heads more than actual job descriptions: Frogman, assassin, special operator.

We envision someone who magically turns up in a dark and dangerous space on the other side of the world and blows up a secret warehouse. However, such fantasies relate to types of covert action rather than intelligence-collecting, which is a C/O's main job description.

Occasionally, the media tries to fill in the blanks with

journalistic reports. They are usually just as wrong as anything from Hollywood.

I entered on duty, or EOD'd, in the CIA's two-year, operations training program in mid-1997 and quickly learned what Case Officers were like.

At the time, I still believed in superheroes. Filled with naïve idealism, I thought that C/Os were a real-life embodiment of the Justice League, with HQS as their storied "Hall of Justice."

Then, I met my classmates.

I'd love to make the feel-good statement that those who EOD at the Agency are supremely qualified Americans who are ultimately corrupted by an oppressive bureaucracy.

But the sad fact is that, despite the rigorous interview process, most C/Os stumble into the career out of sheer luck or bizarre circumstance and end up unsuited for the work.

Being chosen for a C/O position is a lot like winning the lottery. Most applicants don't have an exceptional education or any special experiences, nothing in particular to recommend them for such a unique career. They seem pretty much like everyone else.

For many, the only difference is that, after they get a few years of almost-any kind of experience, they happen to "buy a ticket" by sending in their resume and playing against the million-to-one odds. For the lucky ones, their numbers hit, and they win the grand prize.

Don't get me wrong. Most of my classmates were perfectly nice, patriotic Americans. I'd met them before, or at least people like them, a thousand times in my life, in many different places. They were pleasant to talk to, and we all got along. No major personality issues. None had been fired or arrested—yet. They were just fine.

That was the problem.

Fine was fine for any other job. But we were entering a colossal, almost-mythological, profession. So I expected unprecedented, the best of the best, a batch of new-hire superheroes.

I imagined our class would include explorers and entrepreneurs, adventurers, poets and philosophers, wise academics. Maybe even an eccentric alcoholic. I'd envisioned listening to stories of unique and remarkable—even unheard-of—deeds that gave them something to say about the world.

Instead, I got the following exclamation from a classmate when he heard about my own background: "Wow, you've really got your shit together!"

I had EOD'd with the belief that my type would be the rule, not the exception.

To be clear, this wasn't because I was particularly extraordinary. But my classmates seemed so . . . ordinary.

Most had barely left their comfort zones, had never lived outside the US, couldn't speak a foreign language, hadn't accomplished much to set them apart.

While applicants are required to have good grades, only a few had attended prestigious universities. Not that a diploma is some magic credential. Trust me, I've met plenty of underwhelming Harvard grads. But it's something.

Perhaps most surprising of all, many classmates had little or no athletic ability. I found out later in training that a few—even former military officers—could barely swim.

I believed the CIA would get the best and brightest, but they often don't. Some say that things used to be different, that, at one time, the DO was a bastion of East Coast, blue-blood, Ivy League grads. But even this is a myth. Officers of the past were typically Midwest, white-bread, state college types with a few years' experience in the Army or Marines. Not much has changed.

In the end, I'd busted my tail to join a class of Goldilockses. Not so great and not so bad, but ultimately leaving me no one to look up to, to learn from, to emulate.

Ironically, many of my classmates agreed.

They were happy to tell me they'd stumbled into the career—bored, lost, unhappy in their jobs, they'd submitted an application to the Agency, almost on a whim, maybe late at night, never even expecting a response. They'd applied for all the reasons I'd previously scoffed at others about—a secure government job, decent pay, maybe some prestige and excitement.

And here's the kicker. Even they couldn't understand how they'd been accepted. Most had completed an undergraduate degree and worked an office job for a few years. A couple had done a semester abroad.

That's it.

Yet here they were. *The Chosen Ones*, selected from possibly hundreds of thousands of candidates by the most powerful spy agency in the history of the world.

So what happened? How did they get in?

First, they were relatively safe in the eyes of the Agency.

Not that they didn't have bugs or defects, even deep personality flaws. As we shall see later, the organization kind of likes these things.

But they hadn't broken any really big laws—never tried to overthrow the government, traffic drugs, commit bodily harm to others. Logically, these would have been deal-breakers.

They were also safe since they had passed all the tests and interviews, jumped through the hoops and over the hurdles. In short, they were certifiably "okay." After months and months of microscopic examination, nothing too disturbing had been found. Nothing, as far as anyone knew, that could harm the Agency—or get those recruiters who signed off on them into trouble.

How does someone receive this stamp of approval? Largely by staying in his lane, taking few chances in life, and not doing much out of the ordinary. I suppose, every now and then, they're willing to take a chance on a candidate like me, but clearly not that often.

What happens when an organization hires conventional candidates? They get conventional Case Officers.

As we'll see later, the Agency—like the rest of the country—has become obsessed with safety, almost to a crippling degree. These days, the CIA could also be called "the CYA," partly because of these hiring preferences.

The second reason for my classmates' success was patience—or lack of other options—to wait out the application process, which can take up to a year or more. A former instructor received an offer *five years* after submitting a resume.

Many qualified people are simply not willing to wait that long. Some get better offers in the meantime, while others just drop out of the process.

That leaves those with nothing more pressing in their lives but to wait.

And wait.

And wait, while bureaucratic processes, evaluations, and background investigations take their sweet time to complete.

Perhaps the Agency also sees this period as a kind of test for applicants: How long are you willing to wait? If the answer is "not that long," then you're probably not too committed to the job anyway. After all, the DO entrusts C/Os with enormous power and responsibility. It may well be the most sensitive position in the US government.

That means applicants need the patience and discipline to function in blurry, unpredictable situations where little feedback or supervision is provided. Such situations litter the intelligence field.

Next, my classmates were geographically diverse. Don't forget, Congress has plenty of authority over the Agency's purse strings, even micromanaging—to a shocking degree—its operational decisions through budgetary control. So Senators from far-off Montana or Alaska want their constituents represented. They warn that Georgetown grads from suburban Maryland better not get all those prized positions. Like with college applicants, the (very bright) student from rural Idaho likely has a better shot at getting into Yale than a similarly qualified applicant from New Haven.

A few had been selected for their native foreign language skills. These are necessary, of course, since the DO operates in virtually every part of the world. But such coveted language abilities can come at the expense of other important skills and qualities. Some such officers seemed to be one-trick ponies, more like interpreters than actual Case Officers.

The CIA also wants recruits from a diversity of

professions. So we had former bankers and lawyers, military officers, engineers. And of course, plenty of generalists.

Why don't the best and brightest apply to the Agency?

Well, come on, it's The Age of Individualism. Patriotism and public service are generally not in style these days.

Instead, the truly accomplished prefer to chase the money, rather than serve their country in far-off places. They make their marks in law, medicine, technology—careers that promise the greatest fortunes—all the while assuming that government work offers few financial rewards. We'll see later how wrong they are.

In hindsight, I realize that my confusion about my classmates was just that—mine. It wasn't them—it was me. *I* was the one with the out-of-whack expectations.

This lesson was the start of an education in realism over idealism.

So much myth and legend surround an entity like the CIA, that its people are expected to be special. But the DO taught me, once and for all, that superheroes are fiction. No matter how much we want, need, or love them, they only exist in bad movies and comic books.

C/Os couldn't possibly resemble the hyped-up, Hollywood version of reality. In fact, most of us are the complete opposite. We're just human, all too human.

Lesson Three

A Secular God

It's not just super-strength that will save us. As mere mortals, we crave explanation about the world around us—*what does it all mean*? We seek god-like figures on earth who can guide us, protect us, answer the big questions in life—perhaps even secretly control our lives.

Religion helps fill this void, but let's face it, even in the best religions, most of the good stuff comes in the hereafter. And the notion of God intervening in our daily lives? So medieval.

Supernatural entities, like UFOs and ghosts, have been test-marketed for this purpose. But even these exist only at the fringes of society, far beyond scientific reality.

And in the mythical world of espionage, we have James Bond—a fictitious version of a near-flawless, omnipotent being. Like Jesus, he is both human and divine, risking his life to save us from our sins—or at least the most-evil villains on the planet.

What we need is a real-life, credible alternative. One that places mankind at the center of power, but which is also mighty and mysterious—dare I say, *spooky*?—enough to resemble a religious entity.

Only a few earthly options meet these requirements.

God may have "died" in the late nineteenth century, but He was resurrected in updated form. In my experience, that form is the CIA. In effect, we have anointed the CIA a modern, secular god—an entity to take over the role that religion left behind.

So why did we choose the Agency?

Largely because of the unknown. We Americans want to know about the world around us. If we are not allowed to peer over a wall, we naturally assume something important, even mysterious, is happening on the other side. We are a people fraught with big imaginations.

The CIA is one such wall. Unlike religion, there's no doubt that the Agency exists, but most will never see its inner workings.

There's also no doubt that the CIA collects information—just look at its name. With monikers like "Central" and "Intelligence," the entity must also hold the most valuable information on the planet—which must include *The Truth*. The Truth about the world, how the puzzle pieces fit together. Things we are not allowed to know.

To some, the Agency even performs occasional "miracles," also known as covert action programs, that alter reality and prevent horrible events, such as wars and terrorist attacks.

Unfortunately, the reality is that the CIA produces pretty insignificant stuff. It uncovers few deep revelations (at least revelations that turn out to be true) and even fewer grand truths about the world and its inner workings.

Still, our imaginations are more powerful than reality.

For many, learning such facts is both sad and disconcerting. Some might even refuse to believe them, insisting that, despite all evidence to the contrary, *something just has to be out there*. Even if the CIA went away someday, another organization would surely take its place in our collective consciousness.

Yours truly possessed pseudo-religious feelings about the Agency, which seem ridiculous in hindsight. The night before I EOD'd, I didn't sleep a wink, in part out of fear that I might actually go blind when I walked into the HQS building—as one gazing into the face of God. Fortunately, the unholy reality of its people quickly brought me back to earth.

Perhaps this takes the metaphor too far. But if the CIA is indeed a secular god, then C/Os are its messengers. They report to the main deity, the "Mother Ship," as HQS is ironically known. Society expects them to operate on a higher plane, with greater knowledge, power, and authority. In short, this perception relegates C/Os the task of not only looking after their country, but collecting and preserving The Truth.

Religious symbols, rituals, and overtones at the Agency reinforce this concept. A plaque in the main lobby quotes the Bible (John 8:32): "And ye shall know the truth, and the truth shall set you free." How's that for being subtle?

So much for separation of church and state. But it would appear that this "church" has become a strange part of the state.

How on earth can one question—or for that matter, ever reform—an organization which has proclaimed such a holy mission? Which has established itself the final arbiter and clearinghouse, not just for intelligence, but for truth itself?

I humbly agree with the poetic assertion that "beauty is truth . . ." In our otherwise-phony world, where virtually nothing is what it seems and most everyone wears a front, nothing is more powerful, refreshing—and yes, *beautiful*—than the truth.

Like beauty in a song or poem, you often know truth when you hear it. It's a light but lovely slap on the face, waking you from the nightmarish thought that nothing is real anymore. Nevertheless, truth, like beauty, is still a rare commodity.

So the Agency's search for truth is cloaked as an almost-religious type of quest. Even its name reflects the power of the earthly deity. For what other single word—or in this case, acronym—is so loaded with provocation? Uttering "the CIA" is like taking the Lord's name in vain. It draws immediate attention, cuts through otherwise banal conversations. Officers rarely voice those three tiny letters, especially overseas—they're just too potent.

Incidentally, this may also explain why some insist on dropping "the" in front of CIA, for there is only one such god, negating the need for a clarifying definite article.

Perhaps the most infamous Agency official to ever walk the hallowed halls was the appropriately named James Jesus Angleton (for obvious reasons, his middle name is never dropped). As head of counterintelligence during the Cold War, Angleton's job was to protect the CIA and its flock from evildoers both inside and outside the organization. Although his passion for the work often turned to paranoia, he remained in the position for decades. Given the religious themes at the Agency, his particular name likely ensured some job security—after all, how do you fire a guy called "Jesus?"

During training, we were initiated with pseudo-religious rites and rituals, in addition to the standard hazing practices often related to paramilitary training. One such late-night ritual included being thrown into a van that sped down backcountry roads and came to a screeching halt while an instructor read, in near-pitch-black, an anecdote about a past Agency hero.

Such mystical practices prompted a classmate to mock the instructors by sarcastically exclaiming, "Dance my children . . . dance like the wind!"

The CIA, like an organized religion, is set up as a hierarchy. Naturally, those at the top enjoy offices *at the top* of the Original Headquarters Building, Seventh Floor, where they may peer down at the faithful. Interestingly enough, according to Islam, God and the angels also reside in the seventh level of heaven, resulting in the expression "seventh heaven." The seventh floor provides a respite from the rest of the building, with newer furniture, fresher air, and actual carpeting in the hallways. Other parts of HQS—except the stereotypically more-civilized Europe Division—sport cold, tile floors.

There are more-subtle ways the Agency flaunts its own righteousness, including how it communicates.

A C/O documents street operations using official, computer-based cables. Just like biblical text, this record is meant to be permanent and final.

Remarkably, Agency text also portrays its personnel as nearly infallible. Though other participants, especially agents, may make mistakes and get blamed for things that go wrong, a DO officer never will. A C/O—never ever never—admits guilt or confesses wrongdoing in official cable traffic. He will ignore, exaggerate, even prevaricate, about actual events before doing so.

But he may use coded language when there's no

getting around the fact that, well, mistakes were made. For example, if a C/O simply forgets to conduct an agent meeting, he may characterize the slipup as "a scheduling conflict." Indeed, "cablese," the often-cryptic language used in official documents, can be as hard to decipher as ancient religious text, though some profess fluency in the pseudo-language.

At other times, an officer goofs up by documenting information that is just plain wrong. In these cases, he may use linguistic concoctions to defray the blame. For example, once while in Africa, a station asked for operational assistance while mistakenly indicating that our location bordered a country that was quite a ways away. We pointed out the geographic *faux pas*, prompting the other station to respond that their cable had been "garbled."

In the event of a major operational error, the blundering station will provide a true account of what happened in a backchannel message to those who need to know.

Only those who need to know.

Indeed, if you only read cable traffic without actually visiting the field, you might also conclude that C/Os are the greatest human beings who ever lived—when, in fact, we screw up all the time. But because such mistakes are never really documented, they never really happen.

So much for the beacon of truth.

Despite the hypocrisy, officers will be held accountable for mistakes in the end. Because despite bad behavior, the CIA religion still maintains strict rules that, at least in theory, must be obeyed. And just as God uses confession to ensure that his mortal followers remain faithful, the Agency must also have a way to penetrate your soul.

Enter the polygraph. CIA employees confess their

sins every five or so years to a polygrapher through a routine lie-detector test, all hooked in, strapped to a machine, and watched by security personnel through a one-way mirror. The "box," as it's *affectionately* known, is located down a long, dark hallway, in a small, quiet room, out of earshot of others—where, as in space, "no one can hear you scream." Just walking down that hallway makes you feel like you're on your way to the priest.

At each session, you're supposed to admit everything you did wrong over the last five years, all while trying to prove your worth as a person and employee. As a result, taking a poly is like re-interviewing for your job on a regular basis.

Polygraphers expect plenty of wrongdoing revelations. In fact, there's no passing until they've squeezed enough guilt out of you. "No one is that good," they practically murmur. Everyone tries to hide something.

The entire experience is annoying and belittling and sometimes sickening, but it serves to remind the employee who is really in charge. As a "recovering Catholic," I spent hours in multiple tests, confessing all sorts of irrelevant details that I felt guilty about. Meanwhile, officers who didn't possess much of a conscience typically sailed through the exams, even though they had committed plenty of wrongdoing.

Those were the dark ages.

In the past, the polygraphers yelled and screamed, got in your face, and accused you of the worst possible crimes on earth. In recent years, perhaps for legal reasons, they've stopped such aggressive tactics. They now seem like kinder, gentler enforcers—more New than Old Testament. But don't be fooled. Like many people you know, they've simply switched to more passive-aggressive techniques. And ironically, the bar is now higher, the tests even harder to pass, likely due to recent, high-profile traitors in the Intelligence Community.

Depending on the gravity of your transgressions, you may be given penance. For example, you could be transferred to a job with little responsibility or less access to sensitive information—a place where, if you really were a bad apple, you could do less harm.

Ultimately, though, the CIA, like God, won't forsake you—if you're a staff officer, that is. Heaven help the expendable contractors and dime-a-dozen agents. But as a staff officer, you're fairly safe, barring any mortal sins. Murder will still get you eternal damnation—that is, arrest and termination. Employees have been arrested after walking out of polygraph tests. Those guys are on their own.

The CIA relies heavily on illusion, with Hollywood as a favorite pal. Hell, we would thank the movies for perpetuating popular myths about the Agency and joke about the omnipotence we hadn't actually earned.

HQS telephone operators still tell stories of callers who ask them to turn off listening devices implanted in their teeth. If the operator is feeling playful, she will request the caller's name, pretend to push a few buttons, and report that the device has been turned off.

Foreign countries have bought into the myths as well. A South Asian intelligence officer once insisted that the CIA secretly controlled the weather, and more specifically, the monsoon storms in his country. This was a senior official—imagine the rumors among ordinary folks.

I've even heard tell of foreign agents who glance to

the sky when told they've been terminated—as if ending their relationship with the Agency means being struck down by a bolt of lightning.

Despite all this, there are other ways to view the Agency.

Whether we like it or not, the US has become the stereotypical world police—the teachers in a global classroom full of irresponsible youth. We separate others when they want to fight, and we clean up their messes if they fight anyway. Sometimes, when talking just won't cut it, we step in, even spank our charges with our Armed Forces.

When the US consults with other Western countries regarding the rest of the world, the discussion resembles a boisterous teacher's lounge, full of complaints about this year's biggest troublemakers.

Even on the global scale, school-like cliques exist. Terrorists might as well be the kids who can't get attention until they throw something, hit someone. The Russians are the moody, rebellious teenagers who regularly threaten to burn down the school. And the Third World? They're the ones held back a grade, stuck in a remedial classroom because they need some extra help.

In this metaphor, the CIA plays the giant, global baby monitor, keeping watch over the young'uns to make sure they're behaved—and they don't try to blow up a building or highjack an airplane.

As a side note, the concept of a government acting in a parental role can be seen in other countries as well. Take China, for instance. Its regime considers its people so infantile and treacherous that it rigorously controls what they read, where they go, and who they hang out with—just like a real parent would with his own child.

One way the CIA checks up on the world is by hiring agents to report on potential troublemakers—professional snitches, so to speak. They work the same as those on the playground, ratting out the bullies and those who cheat on their nuclear weapons inspection tests. C/Os love a good snitch—especially those willing to squeal on their government, evil corporation, terrorist group.

These outrageous beliefs about the Agency's powers reveal more about human nature than the reality of the organization. None of them alter the truth about its actual capacity, current operations, or the mortality of its officers.

As far as I can see, there is no god—not here on earth. Neither is the CIA any kind of deity—it's not omniscient or omnipotent, and it doesn't collect, produce, or even attempt to preserve the truth.

Perhaps a short anecdote can make this point.

A classmate and I were assigned to large, African countries on our first tours. Soon thereafter, our bosses left country, and we were put in charge of the stations, despite being fresh out of the gate.

At one point, we laughed about our huge, if temporary, promotions to Acting Chiefs of Station, while simultaneously noting the difference between the perception and reality of the CIA overseas.

Here we were, two young officers in charge of the most important countries in Africa. We were both on our first tours and each had a grand total of three months' experience.

But that's the reality on earth—The Truth, even. We're almost all alone out here. There are no UFOs and no Big Foot—nor anything else, for that matter. The only ones watching over us are first-tour officers.

Lesson Four

Make-Believe

How many typical workdays involve a group of heavily armed "militants" bursting into a classroom and shooting (albeit blanks) into the air, while you're sitting at a desk learning how to survive a terrorist attack?

Or driving around a racetrack as fast as possible to simulate an escape?

Or shooting your way through a kill house to rescue pretend hostages?

Or using an old, beat-up sedan to smash through even older, beat-up sedans to practice breaking a barricade?

Or taking on a band of evil "Nazis" in the middle of the woods? More on them later.

This is how many of our training days began. It was pure, delightful make-believe.

An instructor told us flat-out to cherish our training, for it will be the highlight of our careers. I was surprised by his comment. After all, we hadn't even done the job, been in the field, or seen any real action yet.

In fact, I wasn't excited about the training at all, at first. Like a few others, I came in itching to go overseas. Even without real skills, I was desperate to jump in and get my hands dirty. So the idea of two years of DC area training was kind of depressing. I had waited months and months for this job, years even, and now I'd have to wait even longer to actually do it.

But like all shifts in life, I eventually settled into it. After all, this was the most unique and profound instruction in the world. And while my classmates may have seemed a bit Clark Kent, training made me think perhaps we really could become superheroes.

And the reality is, though truth may be stranger than fiction, fiction is much more fun. The environment is controlled, the narrative scripted, and the ending satisfying and successful. We were always the good guys, and the good guys always won. Hence, training became, indeed, the highlight of my career.

For months and months, the CIA taught us to shoot, throw grenades, even use explosives; to drive under hostile conditions; to detect surveillance and surveil others; to jump out of airplanes; to convince others to break the highest laws of the land; to recruit and handle agents.

There were great expectations for our class.

We entered on duty in 1997, the fiftieth anniversary of the founding of the CIA. As a result, the powers-that-be decided to start the numbering system over again, making us "Class One." It was a brand-new beginning for both the Agency and for us.

For the Agency's part, the previous decade had been riddled with malaise and confusion. The end of the Cold War, severe budget cuts, high-profile traitors, rock-bottom morale, and miniscule class sizes had all taken their toll. Class One represented a renaissance.

This meant we also received a new title. Prior to this time, C/Os-in-training were called "Career Trainees." But the uppity-ups now wanted to emphasize the special nature of the position. We were officially labeled "Clandestine Service Trainees," or CSTs.

That wasn't the end of the changes, as the Agency tried to revive its glory days. Old-school types were hauled out of retirement for leadership positions, including Deputy Director for Operations, or DDO, the most-senior official in the DO. The new DDO reintroduced high-speed elements of training, like jump school, to turn us into the kind of warrior Case Officer that could operate in any environment. Our trainers threw at us nearly every type of operational and paramilitary instruction they could think of.

This revival was a good lesson. The CIA, like the US government as a whole, swings back and forth like a metronome. It is subject to the whims and whimsies of others, both inside and outside the organization, with mood changes depending on the year, the administration, the attitude of the country, world events, and, of course, money allocated by Congress. It vacillates between happy and sad, bold and cowardly, proactive and lazy. Every year, every class experiences a different Agency.

So our timing was pretty good.

From the start, my classmates and I were treated like valuable commodities. The government had invested huge amounts of time and money to bring us on board, and they were gearing up to spend even more to train us—perhaps more money than is allocated to any other profession. Big things were expected of us, and the Agency wanted to protect its investment.

As a result, we were coddled, nurtured even, and kept from the gloomier sides of the organization. The leadership charged us with carrying on the CIA's legacy, preserving its traditions, defending American freedom and democracy. They called us the tip of the spear in national security. The first to go in. The Intellectual Marines.

Thankfully, we bonded as a class pretty easily. After all, we were hired in part for our social skills. It was only natural that we would try them out on each other. Some classmates needed to sniff out the competition, to see what they were up against. Indeed, it became apparent early on that the most-immediate threat, at this stage anyway, wasn't the Russians or the Chinese, but the student sitting next to you who could get what you wanted or make you look silly. So while pleasant with each other as a whole, we competed mercilessly for the attention and commendation of our superiors.

Our class went to happy hour on Friday afternoons. On our first outing, we met up at a popular DC restaurant packed with yuppie lawyers and congressional aides. We huddled around the bar, though our group was large enough to spill into the surrounding area. And there, in the middle of the restaurant, an unknown older man in a suit parked himself on a stool, silent, arms crossed, twenty feet from the actual bar. No one else seemed to notice, but I expect he was our minder, perhaps sent to make sure that, as new and rambunctious officers, we didn't say or do anything provocative, like mention the name of our employer out loud.

Back at HQS, we started off in three-month interims to practice drafting cables, filing papers, and making coffee. Those relatively menial tasks also served as a kind of hazing ritual.

There were other, more playful, rites of passage for

newcomers to the Agency, similar to asking a high school freshman for her elevator pass.

For example, shredder bags are used to dispose of hard-copy cables and documents. When full, they are dropped down a chute in the hallway and then incinerated to make sure the classified contents are destroyed. In one of the rituals, supervisors instructed us new guys to yell our badge numbers when dropping the bag down the chute. It was important, they said, that those in the basement know the officer behind each bag. Yep, Agency humor, but no one ever fell for it.

As cocky, young officers, we reciprocated by playing pranks on our crustier colleagues. During an interim in the East Africa office, a staff desk officer sang out loud, as if no one else were around to hear his annoying melodies. A fellow classmate and I conducted a covert op to shut him up by discreetly calling his office line whenever the singing got bad, then hanging up when he answered. The calls not only temporarily distracted him from the songs, but they drove him crazy when he realized no one was there. A few dozen ghost calls later, he got so frustrated, he had the communications office replace the phone and rewire the entire extension. After a short respite, we began calling him again.

Believe it or not, some classmates didn't pass the hazing phase. To them, clerical work, even temporary clerical work, was far too demeaning, especially given their previous careers. For example, one colleague—the other hired applicant from my Hell Week group—came from a career arguing cases in front of a state supreme court. Another had consulted with a high-powered environmental firm. How could they be expected to make coffee for meetings they weren't even allowed to attend? Each lasted only a month or two before they quit.

More paranoid classmates worried that quitting had been our former classmates' plan all along—they argued that "lawyer" and "environmental consultant" were merely fronts they'd used to gather the true names of everyone in the class to ultimately pass on to a hostile intelligence service.

But in the Agency's eyes, self-termination was just as good as being let go. No matter how it ended, clearly these folks weren't cut out for the job. All the better to weed them out as early as possible before they learn anything truly significant and more money is spent on them.

What these employees didn't understand is that the CIA doesn't care how important you were in your former life. When you join the Agency, time begins again. Like an army recruit, everyone starts at the bottom and must prove themself again in this new life.

Similarly, the Agency never fully trusts anyone. After all, an employee could go bad at any point in time. That means the entire career of a C/O, an agent, even a HQS receptionist, becomes one continuous test, with evaluations every step of the way.

Our interims were no different. Sure, we'd met the entry requirements, but now we faced a whole new set of hurdles.

So the hazing rituals made sense to me. Why waste valuable training on employees who will leave at the slightest inconvenience? How would such employees react in real-life situations when things got really boring—even painful? The Agency was right. Those that dropped out clearly didn't want the job badly enough.

For those of us who stayed, we eventually made it to the next level. At that point, official training began in the special operations course. I have never felt prouder (and more daunted) than the day we arrived at that rural training facility.

For two months, we dressed as soldiers, slept in quonset huts, ruck-marched at dawn, rappelled down walls, fired rifles, pistols, shotguns, machine guns, jumped out of airplanes, drilled tactical driving techniques, practiced land navigation, and romped around the woods. We also patrolled the nearby river all camo'd up, assault rifles hanging off the end of our zodiac boats. The looks on the faces of passing fishermen? Priceless.

Our superiors even required us to walk through a cloud of pepper spray, so it wouldn't come as such a shock if we encountered it during a future civil unrest. A decade later, I swallowed three years' worth of tear gas during the Arab Spring, but I never really got used to that awful stuff.

During the harder days in the heat, when we were covered with ticks and mosquitoes or soaking wet after crossing a stream, one of the instructors reminded us, "Don't worry. You're still getting paid today."

To me, his comments were baffling. Money was the last thing on my mind. I mean, sure, I was sweaty and uncomfortable, but I was living my fantasy. Why would I care about a salary? I felt like a kid getting paid to ride a roller coaster. Hell, I would have gladly reimbursed the Agency for this training.

That being said, I did take to heart another of the instructor's seemingly obvious comments: "Never quit," he told us over and over again. "Never, never, never.

No matter what happens." I still repeat this mantra to myself over twenty years later.

In between these exercises, instructors infused our training with the mystical rites and rituals mentioned earlier. These resembled a kind of mafia-type initiation, so much so that graduates of the Case Officer training program are referred to internally as "made guys."

Another exhilarating course, "Crash and Bang," consisted of two major joys of my life: driving and shooting. We drove fast. We crashed cars. We shot guns—sometimes all at once. I snuck back in line to do the exercises twice. In fact, I loved the experiences so much, I often stayed weekends to explore the facility solo while the others returned home to DC.

Oh, yeah. Did I mention we fought the Nazis?

Our instructors used the fiftieth anniversary milestone to honor our CIA ancestors. That meant magically transforming the entire class into Office of Strategic Services fighters in WWII Western Europe. We were given *noms de guerre* and identity papers used by real OSS officers a half-century earlier. We even carried weapons from the period, including the Thompson, Sten, and Grease Gun.

We spent weeks battling Nazis. By day, we parachuted behind enemy lines, met underground sources, and ambushed enemy convoys.

By night, we pulled guard duty and protected our camp from Nazi scouts and infiltrators played by the real-life guard force on base.

Eventually, our whole class was captured, interrogated, and detained in a prison camp. I'm proud to say I was the only one who escaped—the only one who even tried to do so.

We were fortunate that the paramilitary officer in

charge had an eccentric flair and made scenarios fun and quirky. "C" was a kind of real-world Colonel Flag, straight out of central casting. Somewhat skinny and bespectacled, C made sure we knew that a character from the movie *Heartbreak Ridge* was allegedly based on him.

C threw his heart and soul into designing and executing our scenarios, including dressing up in German uniforms and hamming up every part he played. Not only that, but he blasted the *Mission Impossible* theme song from an old van while we prepared for operations.

After the paramilitary course, we moved on to *The Mother of All Training* and the reason most of us had joined the CIA in the first place.

The legendary basic tradecraft course teaches CSTs the fundamentals of human intelligence operations and how to conduct the full agent recruitment cycle: to spot, assess, develop, recruit, handle, validate, terminate, and re-recruit human sources. It also teaches how to surveil and detect surveillance, which are critical facets of these operations. Every imaginable scenario was covered in the course. We conducted operations ranging from the earliest stage of bumping targets of interest, to developing and recruiting them, to dealing with walk-ins, to handling, turning over, and terminating established agents.

The training repeated itself *ad nauseam*.

By day, we cased operational sites and conducted surveillance detection, including hours of walking and driving. Developmental and agent meetings followed these activities.

By night, we wrote up lengthy, descriptive cables about these events, along with detailed intelligence reports provided by agents, pounding on the keyboard until one or two in the morning.

We did this over and over again, each and every day, for months and months. It was thorough and repetitive and exhausting. There was no *Mission Impossible* soundtrack this time. The course dragged on forever.

That was the point.

Because come on. If you can't prove your resilience in training, no one will trust you in the real world, where you're likely to be alone, without help or trainers checking up on you.

Surveillance detection is a key component of tradecraft, ensuring that operational meetings remain secret, devoid of others who could find out about your meeting or expose the source.

From the very beginning, we were told that if we couldn't detect, we couldn't become Case Officers. So naturally, our entire class was on edge, desperate to prove we could do the job. In my case, detection wasn't as hard as I'd expected. That said, a few of my classmates couldn't hack it.

I began a vehicular route about a quarter-mile behind a classmate and noticed that he had a few cars following him. Back in the classroom, I conferred with him to make sure he'd seen them—they'd seemed fairly obvious to me. To my surprise, he was shocked by my revelation, exclaiming, "I had them on me?!"

Needless to say, the course didn't certify him as a C/O, switching him instead to a similar, but less-operational, position. Ironically, he'd been one of the few Ivy League grads in the class, one who was particularly good at promoting himself—so much so that we'd joked he must be in line to become DDO someday.

But in this line of work, I was learning, educational background possessed fairly little predictive power. One of the few officers not to be certified in the next class was a West Point graduate.

US government trainers also seek to hammer down any nails sticking up, so to speak. They do this by ensuring that every student takes training seriously, ensuring that no one believes they're more important than their work.

One of the ways the instructors attempted to corral the class was to constantly remind us to stop thinking like students and start thinking like Case Officers. I perpetually responded that they should stop treating us like students, and round and round it went.

Because despite our instructors' mantra, we *were* students, which meant we were also obsessed with getting good grades. But as at other institutions, the results didn't always reflect a classmate's actual performance.

For example, while both genders performed at approximately the same level, the female students not only received noticeably higher grades, particularly from the male instructors, but they also received far fewer Less-than-Satisfactory marks, or "Lesters." The female instructors even commented on the apparent bias but refused to play the game.

Why did this happen? Was it a father-daughter dynamic? Part of a traditional role of taking care of the opposite sex? Fear of a sexual harassment or discrimination complaint?

Who knows? It certainly wasn't the women's fault—though some adeptly used their femininity to build "rapport" with their instructors. But such bias happened regularly enough to spark jokes about it. We'd often laugh when a male student did something wrong and was penalized, but a female who did the same thing wasn't even reprimanded. Some of the women actually graduated with unblemished records, without a single Lester.

As the course came to a close, attention turned to our post-graduation careers. Geographical division chiefs performed dog and pony shows for the class to attract the best and brightest students, and we submitted our preferred geographical placement lists.

Africa was at the top of mine. It was the next frontier, I thought, a region I desperately wanted to explore.

Up until the presentations, I was virtually alone in my desire. Only one other student had expressed any interest in AF Division. To most, Africa seemed like a scary place, full of wars, disease, and poverty.

That is, until Chief/AF spoke to us.

His very first words were: "I did three tours in Africa, came home with two hundred thousand dollars, and bought a house with cash." He went on to describe the expat life in Africa, complete with mansions, swimming pools, and even a private tennis court. He said very little about the wars, disease, and poverty—or about the actual work.

The promise of money, luxury, and in fifteen minutes, he'd flipped a switch in our class. Suddenly, many students were jockeying for Africa Division.

These upstart Africaphiles dreamed of riches and the colonial lifestyle—and used their political skills to get what they wanted.

As a side note, a few who were eventually selected by AF Division didn't last terribly long, ironically. One classmate's dream turned into a particular nightmare. During her daily commute in West Africa, she passed dead bodies in the street, some the victims of "necklacing" with gas-soaked, flaming tires. In her non-palatial townhouse, her toilets regularly backed up, as those in charge of emptying the septic tank often just pretended to do their job. In fact, she reported that they only actually emptied it after the contents overflowed onto the floor, and she screamed at them at the top of her lungs. Not surprisingly, she fled back to the First World after just one African tour.

I didn't play politics, promote myself, or try to undermine fellow students. In my mind, those tactics were saved for the opposition, not fellow officers. I believed, perhaps naively, that my skills and experience were enough to ensure success.

I had good grades and took the training seriously. But I was also a smart-ass, sarcastic and sassy, a little too big for my britches.

My immature behavior ruined the impressions I made with some instructors. For example, somehow I had pissed off a senior Africa officer enough for him to recommend that AF Division not pick me after the course was over. Perhaps my mouth had gotten me into trouble again. Or he might have considered me unprofessional because he noticed the holes in my shoes during our personal meetings.

The end of the course finally came—the proverbial day of reckoning had arrived. Most, but not all of us, graduated. And thanks to an ill-timed nap, some of my friends thought I'd been axed.

The program for one of the last days of training included a blissful nothing formally scheduled for the afternoon. Tired from the course, I took full advantage and napped in my room. While I dozed, the instructors assembled the students for an *ad hoc* briefing. They had completed their final evaluations, and they told everyone to look around the classroom. Whoever was present had successfully completed the basic tradecraft course and would graduate. Only later did I learn that my friends glanced around, didn't see me, and assumed I had been voted off.

Lucky for me, I not only graduated, I enjoyed every moment of that snooze.

We had survived one of the most-rigorous training programs in the world—months and months of writing, driving, and assessment. We were relieved, exhausted, and excited for our next steps.

Sadly, the pendulum has swung back in recent years. Soon after we left training, the DO reduced the length of the special operations course and took away elements that were considered non-essential, including jump school. Ironically, these revisions happened right before 9/11, after which C/Os needed high-speed training more than ever.

In fact, as more non-C/Os reached upper management in the DO, senior officials began including those with non-operational job descriptions in the tradecraft course. This decision diminished the status of the program, as more and more Agency personnel brought home a trophy.

But for Class One, almost two years of make-believe was finally ending. We were about to return to the real world.

And as I would soon find out, that old instructor was right. It had been the best part of our careers.

Lesson Five

Purgatory

A senior DO official spoke to our class soon after we EOD'd. He emphasized the exceptional nature of our profession, how our skills set us apart from the crowd. As with special operations forces on a military base, he believed C/Os should be physically separated from the rest of the organization. Some would consider his comments elitist today.

He didn't get his way.

Instead, after two years of being coddled and protected during training, we were ceremoniously dumped into the *general prison population* as another cog in the CIA wheel.

Make-believe had officially ended. The honeymoon was over, and it was now time to grow up and enter the real world. To put all that training and knowledge to good use for the CIA.

HQS acts as the waystation before freshly-minted C/Os head overseas to take part in their assigned missions. Officers can stay anywhere from a few months to a few years before starting an assignment.

Day One was a rude awakening.

After two weeks of leave, every new C/O ritually returns to HQS on the same day, meeting in the CST personnel office. When we returned, the chief summoned us in one-by-one and officially presented our division assignments. We couldn't wait to learn our fates—in which region would we be spending a significant portion of our careers?

Despite the disapproval I'd earned from that senior AF Division officer, I still held out hope that Africa would somehow come through and pick me after all.

No such luck. When my turn came, I was told I'd been drafted by Near East Division. The Near East Division?! I was floored.

NE had been at the bottom of my list.

I knew almost nothing and cared even less about the history and culture of the Middle East, nor did I have any desire to learn Arabic or Farsi. I immediately asked a colleague to switch with me. She just laughed.

But I wasn't kidding.

Largely due to the troubles in the region, NE had become the DO's premier division, taking over the mantle from Central Eurasia after the Cold War ended. And perhaps as a result, it was known for encouraging cowboy-type behavior.

That still wasn't my gig. I didn't think so, anyway.

I would later understand that Fate had smiled on me that day. I hadn't gotten what I thought I wanted, but given what took place over the next twenty years, spending most of my career in NE Division was the best thing that could've happened to me. That division fulfilled my dream of seeing history up close—taking part in it, even—as I worked in places that made the headlines every day.

But I digress.

Returning to that first day back at HQS. After receiving our division assignments, our next step was to march over to our new divisions to receive our job assignments. Still angry with my placement, I walked into NE, flopped into a seat, and asked the head of personnel, "So what does *NE* stand for anyway?"

"Guess you didn't expect to come here, did you?" he asked with a blank stare. "No," I responded. "I didn't." We both stared at each other uncomfortably for several more seconds.

Told you I was great at first impressions.

Then, the other shoe fell.

Apparently, NE needed me so badly, they couldn't offer a single overseas assignment for almost two years. *Two more years of waiting*. Needless to say, at this point, I just wanted to throw up.

I later learned that the selection process had been largely political, rather than what was best for either me or the Agency. As a big, important division, NE had simply demanded another body. They argued their case to the Seventh Floor, insisting that given the scourge of terrorism in the region, they clearly needed an extra officer more than Africa did—even if they had no specific assignment for me.

Just a few weeks earlier, I had been on top of the world, going a hundred miles per hour, euphoric. And now here I was, a hundred miles per hour straight into a brick wall.

I'd be stuck, forgotten, lost in the bottomless pit of assignment-less HQS. No one would even think about me for at least a year, and I'd spend two more years in the DC area. Two more years, when all I'd wanted from day one was to head back overseas.

And that wasn't even the worst of it.

Even though I was officially certified, they say you

never really become a C/O until you go out in the field and do the job—or more specifically, recruit an agent. After two long years of training, I was dying to finally become a real Case Officer.

Instead, personnel instructed me to report to the South Asia desk. After spending perhaps a million dollars to hire and train me, the powers-that-be saddled me with a job that could have been done by a high schooler. My fellow classmates were getting assignments all over the world. Some were scheduled to depart in just months. Meanwhile, the South Asia desk didn't even have an actual *desk* for me to sit at.

So I parked myself for months in an annex office down the hall, twiddling my fingers over the unimportant work I'd been assigned, grinding in my chair, seething and simmering.

CIA Headquarters—where zombies are real, and hope goes to die.

HQS—where a glut of employees, inexplicably, have time to wait thirty minutes in the Starbucks coffee line that snakes around the corner in the food court.

Where most officers sit immobile at their desks, staring at computer screens and sending emails to colleagues a few feet away.

Where those without seniority are forced to park in the dreaded West Lot and trudge a half-mile just to enter the building.

And that's not even counting the joys of living in Washington.

A recent study found that the Washington, DC, area has more psychopaths per capita than any region in the country. The place is infested with an enormous number of muckety-mucks convinced of their own grand importance, with little care for anyone else.

Ironically, the worst part of waiting for an overseas assignment was simply living in my own country.

Back in the office, I got to know mid-and senior-level officers. For while HQS is the starting point for new C/Os, it can also be the end of the line for more seasoned personnel. Some of these folks hadn't left in years.

So let's meet a few mid-level C/Os.

These are the folks who've been in for eight to ten years and have served two or three overseas tours. Now, they're back in the US on an obligatory HQS assignment.

Most are miserable.

They have to commute in that legendary DC traffic and actually pay for things like a house and a car. That's not always easy, given the fact that their salaries took a hit when they lost their overseas bonuses. So many live paycheck to paycheck. They have little to show for the last decade, other than a fresh mortgage, an unhappy spouse, a few spoiled kids, and a closet full of bad suits.

Not only that, but they've now reached middle age, a time for decision-making. Some weigh leaving the Agency because the first few tours didn't live up to their expectations. But where would they go? They may find the work tiresome, but they have few other options that could provide such a life. So they stay put, often for a lifetime, on their way to becoming the proverbial dead wood.

In the mid-level world, there's a good chance they're divorced or creeping closer to it—eighty to ninety percent of C/O marriages fail. This is in part because spouses, who are often just as educated and ambitious as their C/O partners, many times leave their own high-powered careers to join them in, say, Central Africa, where they most likely can't work at all, thus leaving them bored and lonely.

Even when located in the same country, a C/O's work keeps him away from home several nights a week, putting even more stress on families.

As a result, some recommend marrying a fellow officer. You may have the same scheduling issues, and you will spend significant time away from each other. But there's also a chance of a tandem assignment which would allow both of you to work in the same country. And at the very least, each will empathize with why the other is rarely home.

Then, there's the kids.

Many believe that children raised overseas turn out better than those in the US. After all, they're exposed to rich, diverse influences that can broaden their minds. Some do indeed blossom because of these experiences, develop into accomplished adults, attend selective colleges, and start good careers.

For others, this kind of life has the opposite effect. Growing up in a big house full of servants and attending exclusive international schools only spoils them. Their expectations get thrown out of whack, especially after they become adults and return to the States. Growing up with C/O parents who are often away for work doesn't help either. A surprising number of expat kids have difficulty adjusting to the real world while attempting to live up to their previously privileged lifestyle.

The senior officers are even deader wood. Many of their classmates left the Agency years ago. But these officers stayed on, often because they had no other place to go. In the early days, these folks may have been free-spirited, adventurous, interested in foreign cultures and languages. But these qualities have been slowly burned out of them by the suffocating bureaucracy, mindless meetings, and pointless rules and regulations of the Agency. Forced to wear figurative masks and muzzles for years, they become pods, bureaucrats, different people altogether. By now, they're bitter, broken, exhausted shells, fragile wrecks in need of deep psychological help.

Their personal lives are just as wrecked. Many are now on their second or third marriages, paying alimony and child support to multiple exes. Their mal-adjusted kids are ready to enter college, which adds more burden to already-stressed finances. Many times, their offspring wasted the unique opportunities an international lifestyle provided, and so they can't do any better than the local community college.

Some officers respond by retreating like frightened turtles inside their shells, afraid to say or do the wrong things at work. Others attempt to exorcise their pent-up frustrations by acting out at inappropriate times and in bizarre ways. A division chief "joked" to a mid-level C/O at an office party that she was a prostitute.

These officers gave up on the system and the mission a long time ago, but they stick around to qualify for the juicy pension. For many, those retirement checks are all they have to show for years and years of mindless service. They played the game and won—or at least they survived. The sad irony is that their exes will still get half of that pension.

And here I was, knee-deep in misery with them. I considered quitting every single day. The disappointment was overwhelming.

But others around me who knew better advised me to stick it out, that everything goes in waves, especially in this line of work. One day you're down. The next you're up. As such, the government is like the weather: everything can change in an instant if you give it time—and usually when you least expect it.

They were right. The weather changed about three months after arriving in NE Division.

I got a call from a classmate on another desk. He said a job had just opened up in North Africa. A C/O who was scheduled to depart in a matter of weeks had failed his polygraph test, so his assignment had been cancelled. Station needed someone else immediately. Another officer's loss could be my gain. "You interested?" he asked.

I was most-definitely interested, but once again, kind of shocked. Just one day earlier, I had met with the head of personnel to remind him, yet again, of my deep interest in going anywhere in NE Division—especially, North Africa—whenever something opened up. But he hadn't mentioned anything—due to my previous behavior, he wasn't exactly my biggest fan.

Thankfully, my friend gave me the scoop.

And the truth is, many Agency assignments come about this way. DO officers may have little say over where they work and often must wait for something to fall from the sky.

I immediately ran to the personnel office to confirm the opening. The chief was surprised at my question and asked if I were interested in the job. "Yes sir," I said, politely this time. "I would like to go there."

That was all it took. I was granted my first overseas assignment, and just like that, my whole world changed. The clouds suddenly parted, and the sun came out.

I was quickly enrolled in a few short courses to prepare for departure, then provided a new passport and a slew of vaccinations. Ironically, while some of this last-minute training was valuable—who can say no to more driving and shooting?—I wasn't offered a single class covering the history, politics, or culture of my new country.

In fact, most of my pre-departure checklist was *ad hoc* and self-service. Even as a first-tour officer, *I* was largely responsible for navigating my way through the maze of Agency bureaucracy to prepare for my assignment. There's almost no systematic process to follow, despite the multiple hurdles I needed to leap. The right people must sign the right papers at the right time, the right trainings needed completion, and it was up to me to micromanage the process.

It felt as if I were the first person to ever go overseas for the CIA. By the time I stepped onto the plane, it seemed like I'd just parted the Red Sea, and I was finally on my way to becoming a real Case Officer. I snapped on my seatbelt and swore never to work at HQS again.

For my part, I never did.

Lesson Six

PCS

For me, smell is the most evocative sense, closely fixed to my memory and emotions. So while some prefer a bouquet of flowers or freshly baked cookies, as for me, I like jet fuel.

Since I was a little boy, the smell of jet fuel has announced that I am about to embark on an adventure. It is an aromatic declaration that the world is full of wonder and possibility.

In the late nineteen-nineties, I arrived at Dulles Airport in Northern Virginia and breathed in the powerful fumes as planes prepared to depart. After two years, I was finally starting a new journey—a Permanent Change of Station, or PCS, my first overseas assignment at the CIA.

In some ways, this lesson is the trickiest to write. Because I was a unilateral C/O, meaning the local government was not told for whom I actually worked, I cannot acknowledge exactly where I was or describe the work I performed. But I can declare that I finally made it to Africa—the home base for my next adventure. And let me tell you, it was love at first sight after walking into station.

Virtually every career has those special moments—the professional equivalent of making a terrific shot in an otherwise painful golf game. These moments remind you why you're still playing the game and keep you coming back for more.

On my first day in the office in Africa, I was given a drawer in a heavy, reinforced file cabinet to store my classified documents. I dropped some stuff in the cabinet, then curiously examined another drawer. A Hollywood director might as well have staged my scene. I swear, the angels sang.

Two M-4 assault rifles and a steel box with a few hundred thousand dollars were stashed in the otherwise innocuous-looking file cabinet. Throw in a couple of lawyers and we'd have had the full hat trick. And the best part? These essentials were simply tossed in the drawer like any other item, right next to random office supplies. They were just another part of the job. I was instantly smitten with my new life.

That moment was also a jolt to my senses. Somewhere in the transition from training to PCS, I had crossed over. Somewhere over the Atlantic, I had traded responsibility and oversight for freedom and consequences. This was a massive maturation, a giant leap into the grown-up world, into the realm of real people and fragile lives—both of which could be lost from the slightest mistake.

I was out on the frontier now, far removed from the HQS flagpole.

But as always, the magical euphoria didn't last long.

My first Chief of Station, or COS, became the supervisor from hell. "B" was a baptism of fire into the mad world of bad CIA managers.

In some stations, the presence of one or two bad apples doesn't matter much, as they're fairly easy to avoid. But because we were a small office, and B was the boss, he was right there, in my face, every single day.

A hatred for B spurred the rest of station to bond easily. We hung out after work, assigned each other nicknames, and counted the days until B finished his tour the following year.

Nicknames were also assigned to other members of the animal kingdom. When a litter of stray cats made a home on our compound, some were given names since we saw them on a daily basis. The meanest one was naturally named after the boss.

In all fairness, B seemed pleasant to everyone who was not in his chain of command. But if he had authority over you—watch out! As a Vietnam vet, he had learned leadership skills in the military. That meant every lowly subordinate was essentially a young Marine who needed to be broken, to fall in line, and to answer only to him.

Part of me didn't blame him for being that way. I'm sure he'd seen his share of horrors I could never imagine. He deserved a quiet, peaceful place to confront those demons. But that place was not the Agency and definitely not a confined, overseas station.

B had slipped into the DO through the back door, starting his Agency career as an analyst before pulling some strings to switch over to the dark side and become a Case Officer. As a result, he didn't fit in with officers who had been originally recruited for the job.

B possessed bizarre ideas about conducting operations—ideas which seemed to come straight out of the nineteen-fifties—or Amish Country. He was a proponent of trolling, which means wandering around town, hoping to run into someone important; and bumping, which is identifying someone important in advance, following him, and then *accidentally* meeting and chatting him up.

Once cornered, he would present targets with alcohol and dirty magazines, as if a) they were teenagers away from home for the first time, b) B was some kind of pimp, and c) such temptations would prove convincing enough to continue meeting and talking to an American official. Needless to say, none of the tactics ever worked with anyone.

B was also obsessed with safety—at least, his own. Because we were stationed in a high-threat country, the CIA had assigned a full-time security team to protect him. He made a point of reminding his crack squad of guys—who, in reality, did little more than watch TV—that, in the event something horrible went down, *he* was the only one they were to protect. If other station officers were present, he said, push them out of the way to get to him.

Despite his overbearing personality, B taught me a few professional lessons, including one on my very first day: The DO's product, its whole reason for being in business, is our reports. We are judged by all others in the Intelligence Community by this product. Because of this, everything that station disseminates must be flawless, with perfect grammar and no misspellings.

This mantra also translated to making sure we always looked our best, whether or not we were actually *doing* our best. In other words, B emphasized professional style over substance, as style was significantly more noticeable and could make or break a station's reputation.

This lesson also served as my introduction to the COS as politician. In time, I learned that many chiefs obsess over presenting a polished appearance, largely to dissuade higher-ups from closer examination of their often-messy operations.

Soon afterwards, I learned a more cynical lesson. B literally instructed me to make every operational decision as if I were to explain said decision to Congress someday. How's that for "Welcome to the field?"

While B's attitude baffled me at the time, I'm sad to say that as years passed, I realized that his comments do, in fact, reflect how the CIA is run, both then and now. Decisions are often based on the assumption that not only will the operation fail, but that the officers involved will also be blamed for its inevitable failure. As a result, operation planners, spouting off like legal experts, prepare their alibis well in advance—which explains why so few cutting-edge operations are even attempted these days.

CIA operations have devolved into a paranoid game of "Gotcha!" in which each player must constantly watch for any kind of reckoning that could question, punish, or make them look bad.

This fear is largely based in self-preservation. Officers know that management will not stand up for them when operations go bad. C/Os today are even encouraged to purchase professional liability insurance to defend themselves if outcomes result in legal actions.

Such lessons came in handy early in my tour. You see, by the time a manager reaches the height of COS, he has learned all about Agency bureaucracy, including how to use—and abuse—the system to his advantage. Using the cover of "HQS Consultations," B regularly escaped from that hardship post to far-more-comfy Washington, leaving me the cons. Within the first three months of *my very first tour*, I was running the show as Acting COS.

I joked that—finally!—I would live my dream of

communist dictatorship. I could now force my subordinates to dress in uniform, salute their dear leader, and sing songs in my honor.

But such rantings were merely a satirical play on the Hollywood definition of "CIA Official Overseas."

In reality, the average COS has minimal power. In some respects, she is just a more senior functionary in a governmental bureaucracy. That, and all blame settles on her. So basically, it sucks being the boss at the CIA. There are almost no upsides—other than a fatter paycheck and a bigger house. But there are more than enough downsides—more responsibility, ridiculous personnel issues, and that pernicious game of Gotcha!, to name a few.

Such a backwards system also helps explain why Agency management has little appetite for taking risks. If I did well, few rewards, or even congratulations, would come my way. COSs typically receive feedback only when operations go toes-up. So most of these career bureaucrats learn to focus on the one prize they know will come their way if they can simply survive—a big fat green pension.

Needless to say, I didn't live out my dictatorship dreams, and eventually, we all survived B. He went on to a plum follow-on assignment, largely because he had accomplished little but also hadn't made any major mistakes—that, and most of the cables that station sent were error-free.

We breathed a sigh of relief and threw a blowout wheels-up party, made even more joyous upon hearing that B's temporary replacement would be his complete opposite.

We received word about "K's" personality a few weeks before he arrived. He was a "Terminal-14,"

PCS

meaning that even after slaving away in the DO for years and years, he was destined never to become senior management. This sad fact supposedly stemmed from his unprofessional attitude and disdain for protocol.

Internal intelligence about an Agency officer is called a "Hall File," a clever term for an informal, collective reputation based on the mutterings of peers. Hall Files contain valuable insights about what a C/O is really like—is he a crank, a suck-up, a superstar, a failure, or even a psychopath? And bottom line—will we like her?

Hall Files are far more important than actual, documented performance because they are based on raw, personal assessments by trained professionals. While certainly subjective, they address a C/O's reliability, intellect, and personality—bare-bones traits rarely noted in more-sterile, official performance reviews.

In truth, K's insouciance was equated with insubordination by his own supervisors, which reflects a basic instinct of Agency managers, especially those with military backgrounds. If CIA managers detect little to no fear or anxiety in their subordinates, they assume said subordinates are both disrespectful and out of their control—which drives them crazy.

So on paper, K was an insubordinate failure.

But K's Hall File revealed that he was, in fact, beloved by his peers.

This was partly because the man possessed a twisted sense of humor. Once, during a weapons course, a CIA security officer asked, "And where do you live?"

"Europe," he responded curtly. "I can't stand Americans."

In short, K was a California boy who hated formality, phoniness, and following the rules.

He was the perfect antidote to B's venom.

Sometimes, K simply forgot to follow the rules. The guy's arrival at station was delayed because it didn't occur to him that he needed a visa to enter the country. Though he realized his mistake before the flight, he had to wait an extra week for his application to be processed.

The day he finally arrived, we put some of B's beers and magazines originally intended for local targets on K's desk. Not knowing the security code, K knocked on the outside door, and I let him in. He briefly introduced himself and strode into his new office, leaving us confused and fearful we'd received bad intel—that K was not, alas, some easy-going *bon vivant* and the answer to our prayers.

Just then came the crrrack of a beer tab, and when I entered his office, K was enjoying a cold one, his feet on the desk and a *Playboy* magazine wide-open on his lap.

It was going to be a good summer.

K was in charge, but we hardly knew it. He let us work with minimal supervision. He didn't need to lord over anyone to prove his authority. In fact, his nonchalance led some to believe he didn't care much about operations. He did. But to K, Agency business was a thinking-man's job, requiring contemplation, not a military deployment packed with snaps to attention.

Perhaps more importantly, K temporarily renewed my faith in the Agency and its management—at least, he gave me hope that there were still protagonists out there. B had almost convinced me to leave, but K persuaded me to stay.

When it came to operations, K was, perhaps predictably, a little uneven. On the one hand, his carelessness resulted in a trusted asset quitting—though, in reality, that asset's reporting wasn't that great anyway. But on the other hand, he showed such extreme care and concern when reviewing contingencies for a complex operation that I jokingly asked, "What should we do if there's a nuclear attack?"

But like all good things, the summer eventually ended, and a permanent replacement arrived. A wise, old-school type, "J" had assisted in winning the Cold War, and we nicknamed him "Dad." He was highly skilled and intensely loyal to his people, but he had a volatile temper that erupted at any kind of betrayal.

Like K, J also possessed a wicked sense of humor. When addressing the status of his family in an admin cable to HQS, he wrote dryly, "I must now bring up my wife, *as unpleasant as that subject may be . . .*"

J taught me lessons about DO operations—most notably, he shoved me further into the realism camp by pointing out that, while station reporting was indeed our product, most of it made little difference to national security and likely wouldn't even be read. He added that, while the information was nice to have and proved we were earning our pay, the vast majority of it was meaningless.

Eventually, I finished my two-year tour and returned to DC the summer of 2001.

I was at HQS when the 9/11 attacks occurred. Worried that our building would be the next target, my coworkers and I scrambled to the parking lot where we waited and watched until management finally told us to go home.

A few weeks later, I boarded a plane to join The War on Terror in South Asia. At this moment in history, no more exciting place existed in the entire world.

We were a big station, full of young and aggressive officers out to seek revenge and make a name for ourselves. With little social life, we had limited distractions. For two years, life was work—and there was plenty of it.

For me, it was a baptism of fire. I cut my teeth in that station, learning more operationally than most will in an entire career. My colleagues and I worked every day and were on the street almost every night. We were overloaded, exhausted . . . and exhilarated.

The station bullpen, where the younger C/Os sit, was a virtual salon of politically incorrect sarcasm, wit, and wisdom on virtually any topic under the sun. Looking back, those conversations would have gotten us kicked out of country (and perhaps the organization) in today's CIA. But back then, we were feisty, cocky, unafraid. And while I wouldn't have trusted the other C/Os to have my back, they definitely added education and entertainment to the office.

The COS must've suspected that we were an unruly bunch because he dropped in from time to time to say things like, "I wish I had a camera in here just to keep an eye on everyone." We'd inevitably respond, almost in unison, "Oh, God, no. It's a good thing—for all of us—that you don't."

The bullpen was also a generator lab of operations. By day, we brainstormed how to go after important targets, and by night, we applied those very ideas.

An entire career later, after working with more than a hundred C/Os in over a dozen stations and bases around the world, I can count the number of smart, capable DO officers on two hands.

Most of them were in South Asia at that time.

In all fairness, this tells you that performance is, at least partially, based on occasion—that the right situation can bring out the best in people. Like an actor in a once-in-a-lifetime movie, the role often makes the performance. South Asia made everyone step up their game, molding a few of us into exceptional officers.

For a short period after 9/11, the operational environment was virtually wide-open. The country wanted vengeance, and the Agency was ready to comply. We were given long leashes, with the go-ahead to try almost anything possible to get access to valuable sources. We rarely asked for permission in advance, merely reported any successes to management the following day.

And there were plenty of them to report. My colleagues and I were personally behind many of the counterterrorism-related headlines that ran in the newspapers every day—headlines and work that now make up a significant part of Agency history.

From South Asia, I was assigned a relatively pleasant gig in Eastern Europe. Even with its own decaying economy and existential political problems, the country won the trophy for the nicest place I ever worked—I drank potable water from faucets, sat outside in public parks, never heard a single explosion for two years. I didn't even carry a gun.

But that assignment taught me the following lesson: The nicer the place, the worse the people in the office, and vice versa. Eastern Europe was just too comfortable for my taste. Countries like that attract personnel who prioritize safety and self-satisfaction over action and adventure—those who join the profession for personal gain, with little regard for either the job or the mission. Those weren't my people.

So after leaving Europe, I stuck mostly to war zones, combat zones, and hardship posts in Africa and South Asia. Prior to 9/11, a few of these posed as relatively safe, family-friendly countries. But in the last two decades, they have become increasingly dangerous, one-year unaccompanied tours.

Along the way, I witnessed wars, coups, rebellions, revolutions, terrorist attacks, and history-making elections. For nearly twenty years, I never worked in a single country that could be described as safe, peaceful, or prosperous. Wherever I went, something bad happened—even if the tour didn't start out that way.

For example, after years of living apart from my NGO-worker wife, our jobs finally synced up in the same North African city. Part of me was excited. Another part of me felt the need to warn her of the apparent curse I bring to countries—things often turned chaotic upon my arrival.

I joked that there would probably be shooting in the streets soon after we arrived, and we both laughed.

Six months later, the Arab Spring erupted.

We saw and felt that revolution every day for almost three years. Civilian mobs ran wild, set up checkpoints, and burned government buildings. Police responded by clouding the air with an almost-permanent fog of tear gas. Most non-essential station personnel were evacuated, and those that remained were locked down, unable to find out what was really happening on the street.

Later, upon taking an assignment in East Africa, I learned that there are some sad exceptions to the "nicer-the-place" lesson.

Africa, especially during the Cold War, had a notorious frontier mentality. The social and political instability of the region created near-constant operational opportunities for hungry C/Os to make a name for themselves. An added bonus was that in the midst of decaying capitals and governmental collapse, both foreign and local officials often let their guards down. This left C/Os freer to do their operational work than in, say, Europe.

But those days are long gone. Even in Africa, C/Os now rely on corporate, self-promoting personas to impress their higher-ups and advance their careers. In other words, cowboy hats have been replaced by suits and suspenders, and a typical AF station now resembles a high-powered law firm.

At least there are officers still willing to work in Africa.

From Day One, the Agency demands that the needs of the service come first—that C/Os must be available for worldwide assignment. But the reality is that some officers simply refuse to work in a developing country, forget about an actual war zone. These thin-skins will only serve in Western Europe or East Asia—in those places where they studied and vacationed and dreamed of joining the Agency in the first place. Naturally, they imagined themselves reliving those experiences, walking cobblestoned streets and sipping tea in fancy cafes. To save a little face, a few officers use the lame excuse that their spouses won't let them take a hardship assignment.

Ironically, this risk-aversion became a source of disappointment once those officers got overseas, even if they did land their dream assignments. After all, they were on vacation the last time they visited. But they're not on vacation anymore. They came to work. And Europe isn't quite the same sitting in an office all day and plodding the streets at night.

Paradoxically, while these officers may have felt safer and more comfortable in the First World, their lives suffered in other ways.

Notably, their operations paled in comparison to those in the trenches, leading me to another conclusion: the nicer the place, the worse the work. Developed countries typically host enormous, hierarchical stations with lots of protocol but little work. These offices are holdovers from the Cold War, when those who served in them conducted actual operations. Nowadays, any high-speed operations go to the most-senior officers, while those at the bottom of the totem pole can feed on the crumbs. In fact, a classmate served his first tour in Europe and confessed to me later that he didn't handle or recruit a single asset for three years. As a result, he was far behind colleagues who kick-started their careers in less-stable parts of the globe.

In contrast, hardship stations are famous for turning over complex cases to first-tour officers. Bam! Right off the plane, you're handed the most senior, sensitive agent on the books. It's the station's way of throwing you into the deep end to see if you'll swim. And why not? After all, every fresh face is a certified Case Officer—so go do the job. Perhaps not surprisingly, these rookies often had more energy and creativity than their older, "wiser" counterparts.

Socio-economic conditions also make softer stations more difficult to operate. DO officers thrive in countries with weak governments and bad infrastructure. In such places, they can conduct operations fairly easily, as the locals are less likely to pay attention—either because they're incapable, or because they have far worse concerns to think about. C/Os also thrive in countries where poverty and corruption make the locals, well, more corruptible, and therefore prone to recruitment.

In contrast, safe, stable, wealthy countries already have capable intelligence services with firm control over their turf. This means they're vigilant about any threats to the *status quo*, including any unusual behavior, which makes things tricky for those involved in espionage.

Despite the downsides, the poshest countries still attract heaps of applications for every available position. But as with ambassadorships granted to big-money donors, such choice assignments often don't go to the most qualified personnel. Instead, they're doled out to officers with friends in high places or older officers as so-called retirement tours, swan songs for the seniors who have towed the line for decades.

Lesson Seven

What Would You Say You Do Here?

We all use human intelligence more than we realize. We possess sources in our personal and professional lives that provide information, warn of potential dangers or opportunities, and answer our questions and concerns. Friends, family, colleagues, neighbors, even random strangers, may serve these purposes. Most are under no obligation to share any information, however. And as in espionage, some of our sources are more reliable than others.

Collecting from human sources is also a familiar profession. TV journalists and newspaper reporters are two examples of overt collectors. These professions don't typically use secret sources, though they may have to protect source identities if they provide sensitive information. Still, they can't legally pay sources or ask them to break the law.

The DO elevates this collection process to a whole new level.

C/Os establish formal operational relationships by recruiting their sources. They handle these agents clandestinely because each agent is committing espionage by providing protected information to a foreign government. C/Os compensate sources for the work they do and the risks they take, while employing operational tradecraft to keep everyone involved safe.

(If you wonder whether this lesson reveals too much, trust me, the Agency's own website provides enough intimate professional details to make any C/O blush.)

A source is also called a "case," which explains the name of the profession. A clandestine meeting with an agent, or indeed the handling of the case from beginning to end, is an operation. Therefore, Case Officers are also Operations Officers. Because they collect human intelligence, C/Os are formally referred to as "Core Collectors." Most simply prefer the C/O moniker.

C/Os debrief their agents at these operational meetings, assuage their security concerns, pay, task, and praise them for their work. Most agents pass intelligence, though some provide services, such as access to hard-to-reach targets or the use of their residence to hold operational meetings.

Most agents are men. This is because most targets—those with access to important information—are men. After twenty years as a C/O, I only ran across a small handful of female sources, though this will likely change in the future. And truth be told, agents in more conservative parts of the world often prefer to work with men.

Still, male developmental targets—even in the same parts of the world—may prefer women. That's because, while working to recruit a developmental, a C/O showers her target with care and attention. She takes a deep interest in his life, flatters him constantly, invites him to dinner alone, to out-of-the-way places, asks him to keep their relationship discreet, and engages in highly personal conversations. Who wouldn't love that?

Indeed, such attention is so personal and unexpected, some developmentals mistake it for physical attraction.

In fact, the female C/O may need to have an awkward heart-to-heart to bring her developmental back to earth. In response, the developmental may react with sadness or confusion, might even walk away. Hopefully, however, he will see other advantages to the relationship and continue to meet with her professionally.

None of this proves that agents are more reliable than, for example, open sources used by the media. In fact, both types may use the relationship with their handler "to influence as well as inform," ultimately passing information to advance their own agendas.

Back to that biblical quote in the HQS lobby for a minute. To me, the implication that intelligence—in this case, raw data collected from an asset—is on par with the truth seems strange. As in a journalist's story, an agent's information may simply consist of what one person heard from another. In this sense, human intelligence could also be referred to as "professional gossip." Oftentimes, an asset doesn't enjoy direct access to the original source of information—most likely, he's sharing details he's heard second-or third-hand. And when it comes to human intelligence, each participant has their own context, culture, and reasons for sharing information. As a result, the final product can end up far removed from any kind of truth.

In fact, problems may exist even when a source does have first-hand access to the information. For example, I handled a well-placed South Asian with direct access to his country's leadership. Station was thrilled that the US government, in theory at least, was tapping into the intimate plans and intentions of the most powerful people in that land. I later uncovered, however, that the very same leadership likely knew our trusty source enjoyed *some kind of relationship with the Americans*. So in hindsight, everything that he told me became suspect since he (and indeed his leaders) may have actually used our relationship all along to pass favorable information about that leadership.

Long story short—intelligence is never cut and dry.

Some in the business, however, contend that vital, sensitive information is best obtained by paying clandestine sources. Such information must be important and sensitive, they argue, because the sources are secret and salaried.

But the expectation that recruited foreign assets will produce reliable information is riddled with problems.

To begin with, CIA intelligence is only as good as the agents who report it. But *every agent is a traitor*. By their very decision to commit espionage for the CIA, they have proven, ironically, that they can't actually be trusted. Dante went so far as to throw traitors to the lowest circle of Hell—where the Devil himself lived.

Sure, some agents simply chose to work for *the good guys*, to stand on *the right side of history*. A few such sources are actual, *bona fide* heroes, representing the dramatic difference between success and failure in American foreign policy. But most have chosen to cooperate out of basic self-interest—i.e., money—rather than some kind of ideological conviction (no matter what they tell you).

Agents enjoy their CIA salaries—though they're often miniscule—and they'll do whatever it takes to keep them. So they tell their handlers what they want to hear and make up stories when there's nothing to tell.

On a personal level, Case Officers may actually grow to like certain assets—especially if they recruited them. The DO sometimes refers to agents as "partners"—even "heroes"—when they're feeling generous. But in most cases, C/Os, for the reasons described above, don't trust them all that much.

Also, C/Os never forget that most agents are foreigners. They may be helping the US government, but at the end of the day, they don't owe any allegiance to their handlers or the US—or, for that matter, their own home countries. By virtue of their chosen profession, they've proven they can be bought by the highest bidder.

Unfortunately, trust and honesty are critical components of the sensitive and dangerous C/O-agent relationship. For example, we relied on our sources to pass factual information, to provide accurate details about where they got that information, even to admit when they were under suspicion of spying at their work. But how could we expect such values from agents (and as we will see later, many C/Os) who were so deeply flawed?

Still, despite their flaws, agents are the lifeblood of the DO. The acquisition of new sources is essential to its existence—and the source of most of its glory.

Recruitments are the single most important yardstick for measuring a Case Officer's performance, so the pressure to seal deals can be overwhelming. For some, it becomes an all-consuming, existential obsession, the only thing that really matters—especially for first-tours and those who can't seem to pull the trigger. After all, like detecting surveillance, if you can't recruit, you can't be a real Case Officer.

Interestingly, the corporate espionage film *Wall Street* includes an entertaining depiction of the agent recruitment cycle, as Michael Douglas hires Charlie Sheen to collect insider information on companies he wants to buy.

Such a professional barometer is not that unusual. Like arrests for an FBI agent or confirmed kills for a soldier, virtually every political/military career boasts quick-and-dirty performance markers.

At the CIA, it's scalps.

When I finished an overseas assignment, my apparent success or failure would be summed up in a one-word answer. The questioner inevitably asked how many recruitments I racked up during the tour, and my entire operational ability would be instantly measured by that simple response.

Unfortunately, recruiting sources in the real world is hard—no, I take that back. Because recruiting *good* sources is hard.

Why?

First of all, they're hard to find. Americans don't possess natural access to people of operational interest—especially when they're located in hard-target, denied-area countries, where crucial operations take place. In fact, such foreign officials are usually forbidden from even talking to Americans, let alone meeting them outside work, without official permission from their employers.

Sure, we occasionally ran into a foreign diplomat or local counterpart at a social gathering, but these were usually the leftover dregs that had already been picked through by other officers. Really important potential agents don't share common friend groups with Americans or hang out at a favorite watering hole. The CIA usually relies on these hard targets volunteering to them.

Secondly, most people, even under the most-oppressive

regimes, have a difficult time betraying their homeland to commit espionage. Whether out of fear of the consequences or loyalty to country and kin, finding someone willing to break this fundamental allegiance is rare.

And if a person actually has access to important information, he's probably no slacker. Most likely, he holds a pretty good position in his government or terrorist group and is therefore less likely to risk losing everything for a relatively small amount of money.

This means developmental operations demand an abundance of time, patience, legwork, and the ability to take constant rejection. In most cases, the stars must be aligned just right to find and recruit the kind of person who can actually satisfy the CIA's requirements.

There are, of course, more-arrogant officers who believe that almost everyone's recruitable, that everyone can be gotten with the right approach. In my experience, that belief often applies to residents who don't have enough to eat, in regions where nation-states are a relatively new concept, and within countries where people don't share a strong sense of citizenship. Yet as one travels north and west in the world and national loyalties become more firmly entrenched, recruiting becomes harder.

In the end, the product, rather than the salesman, seals the deal in most recruitment transactions. Officers don't possess super-heroic qualities—or even many special skills. The real ingredients that make human intelligence work are the power and influence of the US, coupled with an agent's desire to be on the winning team—with a healthy dash, of course, of salary mixed in. In this sense, a recruitment often resembles a luxury car sale—in most cases, the Ferrari sells itself.

So what inevitably happens in this high-pressured world of competitive espionage where recruiting is everything?

Case Officers cheat. They gin up fake recruitments and phony agents—and they often get away with them.

It turns out, C/Os really do lie, cheat, and steal after all—yep, just like their agents.

In all fairness, such shameful behavior doesn't happen all that often, but it exists. I witnessed the after-effects of one such case first-hand soon after arriving at station.

It all went down as a senior-level colleague was finishing his overseas assignment. He was up for promotion, but he hadn't brought any new sources on board for a while. So in the final months of his tour, he fudged a recruitment by asking a foreign counterpart with whom he met regularly on an official basis to continue seeing him in the same capacity, to continue talking about the same topics . . . blah, blah, blah. To which the counterpart easily agreed, since he had no idea what his friend was really up to. The C/O got him to say things like, "Sure, I like you. Of course, I'll keep seeing and working with you."

Cha-ching! That was all he needed.

The C/O wrote up the whole thing in official traffic as the acquisition of a new source and initially received credit for it. In hindsight, it was a deviously clever ploy that also required the creative writing skills necessary to make an otherwise-standard liaison discussion seem like an agent recruitment meeting in the cable to HQS.

So when the time came for the C/O to punch out and turn the ostensible agent over to his replacement, the meeting, predictably, didn't go so well. The "source" didn't understand—let alone, agree to—any of the secret commitments he had allegedly made, which must be reviewed in front of the incoming officer. At that moment, the whole charade collapsed in an awkward and embarrassing way.

An official internal investigation was eventually launched, and a lengthy—and graphic—report produced and disseminated. Another colleague said it best—the report was "like reading porn."

But no matter. By the time the truth came out, the devious C/O had already secured his promotion, flown out of the country, and been assigned a nifty follow-on tour. I watched his replacement spend the rest of his own tour cleaning up the mess.

In another case I heard second-hand, a C/O's freshly recruited asset *mysteriously* disappeared just before he was to be handed over to a new officer, which at least avoided an awkward and embarrassing turnover meeting. This time, the C/O had also been "paying the agent" for months, so he not only received credit for an apparently phony recruitment, but he had also pocketed thousands of dollars from the fake agent's salary.

While these are likely extreme cases, most C/Os take the more benign, but almost-equally-as-harmful path of going after low-hanging fruit.

At the start of my career, I'd be impressed with heroic stories of officers who collected seven or eight scalps in a single two-year tour. I later learned that many such recruitments were worthless.

In the "low-hanging fruit" strategy, C/Os pursue low-level foreign targets with access to information that looks sensitive on the surface but is actually pretty meaningless. These targets represent the easy-pickings that C/Os know they can get, and in a place like Africa, you can recruit these sources by almost literally offering a cab fare home.

In training, we laughed about targeting Canadian Third Secretary diplomats. The joke was funny, because not only do we not target Canadians, but choosing such a low-level one would also be absurd. In the real world, however, such folly wasn't that far from the truth, and most C/Os simply recruited measly, half-ass sources. As a result, measly, half-ass sources now describe the vast majority of DO assets.

This practice falls into the realm of the time-honored tradition at the CIA, and indeed the US government in general, of passing the trash and screwing your neighbor—in other words, keeping up the appearance of quality work by propping up this person or that program, while secretly praying they stay intact until you can hand the problem to the next guy. After all, *everything seemed fine* when you were in charge of the project. It'll become someone else's headache after you've safely departed.

I've taken over cases from such *superstar* recruiters—cases that splinter even as the recruiter's plane leaves the airport.

One such case was a low-level South Asian extremist. It didn't take long to uncover the fact that he was a decoy sent by the local government to feed us false information and learn how we operated in the country. Sheesh.

I found him out not by using remarkable interrogation skills, but by simply asking the agent a few questions about his background and pointing out some apparent inconsistencies in his information—typical questions his recruiting officer should have posed. Instead, he had simply taken the asset's word as truth—that, or he'd been too lazy or embarrassed to dig deeper. The agent cracked within a few meetings and admitted everything. *Quelle surprise.*

In hindsight, I realize the power of my general disinterest. I wanted the agent to be successful, of course. But I hadn't recruited him, so I wasn't emotionally vested in his success. Instead, I could rely solely on the reality of the case, and the house of cards came crashing down.

In this game, many officers take easy ways out because of the overall emphasis on short-term gains, risk aversion, and quantity over quality. Recruiting a high-level agent with significant access to meaningful information can take a long time, but the boss—and HQS—want results and verifiable progress now. Within the general CIA culture, it doesn't make sense to waste valuable time and energy on a case that may never pan out. After only a few months, most bosses will expect real headway. If that hasn't yet happened, he may conclude that the developmental just isn't worth it. And if that happens, it's time to fish or cut bait—a common expression reflecting the culture of short-term thinking within the organization. In most cases, if success is still unclear, he cuts bait.

And here's the other thing. Even in legitimate recruitments, agents are not particularly effective at doing what they're hired to do—that is, report credible, well-sourced information that's useful to the US government.

Why not?

First of all, as I mentioned previously, handlers want to believe their assets—especially those they recruited. As we learned in the last example, this means they're less likely to vet them or their information too hard. Because come on. Nobody enjoys admitting failure—nobody wants to concede that an agent lies or gives bad information. The way the system works, every C/O needs a certain number of recruitments on the books to prove to the boss she's doing her job. So C/Os naturally err on the side of selling their own assets and developmentals, making him—and, therefore, themselves—look good.

But even if C/Os didn't recruit the asset in question, Americans—even American Case Officers—have a natural tendency to believe what others tell us. We assume that because of our fellow humanity, our agents will share our values, no matter how ridiculous such a notion seems to other countries.

But critical thinking—put more bluntly, a healthy dose of skepticism, even cynicism—may be the most important skill in this business, largely because the vast majority of agents, developmentals, and especially walk-ins—virtually anyone you talk to in the espionage business—are simply full of crap.

In the end, they're merely trying to sell you something, and they know that the better the product sounds, the more you will pay, in one form or another. So they fib, fudge, deceive, distort, fabricate, exaggerate, prevaricate—repeatedly, constantly, early and often, until it's insulting to your intelligence every time they simply open their mouths. Their deception is perhaps the only constant in the otherwise upside-down, unpredictable world of espionage. So to be an effective officer, you need to be able to pick out the real from the fake.

But that isn't what's taught in training. C/Os are merely fed information from make-believe sources. Few exercises forced us to confront deceitful agents and developmentals, to think critically, to vet them and their information. Of course, real, effective validation takes loads of time—and there's never enough of it in training or the real world. Most C/Os merely report what an agent said, cross their fingers, and hope for the best—or, more likely, simply forget about it.

One way to vet an asset is through operational testing. In this technique, the C/O tries to determine whether the asset's qualities—honesty, loyalty, reliability—are genuine, while clandestinely employing a real-world scenario.

Remember that I mentioned I dated a Russian billionaire's daughter in grad school? Even she once ops tested me at her home. She complained that she was cold and asked me to get her a blanket. The blankets were on the top shelf of the closet. After I pulled one down, I noticed a stack of hundred dollar bills on another shelf in the same closet. I was initially taken aback, but knowing her family's wealth, didn't think too much of it. In hindsight, she had obviously staged the scene to see if I would swipe some cash. And indeed, her mood noticeably improved when she later read the favorable test results—that is, verified that none of her money was missing.

Ops testing an agent whom you may see for only a few hours per month and who doesn't even live in the same city, however, is complicated and time-consuming and requires lots of extra paperwork—which C/Os detest more than anything because it's dull and bureaucratic.

So vetting a source has turned into a box-checking exercise—and a low priority one at that—that only becomes important when a source's clearance is up for renewal. The rest of the time, C/Os couldn't care less. They'll just pump out whatever is told to them—with little concern for whether any of it is even true.

And the Agency loves it.

Despite all the credibility problems, the CIA keeps pushing for more and more reporting.

While recruitments are the most important number in this business, the second-most important statistic—and maybe the only other one that matters—is the number of intelligence reports a C/O and station disseminate.

The Agency will deny this fact in one breath, while regretting its existence in the next. As an East African COS declared after his station produced its highest number of reports ever in a month: "It's not just about the numbers. But as we all know, it's just about the numbers—so thank you so much for setting this record!"

The First Rule of Intelligence Collection is that you must feed the beast—dumping as many reports as possible into the system in order to prove you're working hard.

The pressure to produce anything is overwhelming. While it's scary to admit, many stations would rather report information they think is dubious or even untrue than to allow for crickets. Perhaps it hearkens back to that Protestant work ethic, but producing nothing is actually considered worse than getting something wrong. In other words, the appearance of laziness is a greater sin than incompetence.

So CIA intelligence is only as good as its agents—and its Case Officers. C/Os must also be highly skilled. After all, you can have the best agent in the whole world, but if his C/O can't meet him securely and debrief him effectively, it can add up to nothing.

A C/O's job is simple but not easy. In other words, there aren't any complex math or physics equations to calculate—in fact, there are actual children's books about spying that contain most of the essentials, along with colorful pictures. However, an excruciating number of details go into conducting a successful operation and producing a quality product. And missing just one of these details can make the whole thing go south. So the Agency's a good place to work, if, like me, you're a little OCD.

It's also a good place for linear thinkers. In most (but not all) cases, operational events proceed in a certain predetermined order. C/Os must first lay down a foundation and check certain boxes before moving forward with a developmental. Ideally, these events build upon themselves to a climax, which, in this case, means recruitment.

A capable C/O must also have many generalist-type traits. A partial list of handling skills includes natural curiosity, strong focus, street smarts, good judgment, love of travel, language skills, thick skin, excellent memory, attention to detail, awareness of surroundings, good writing skills, goal-orientation, an ability to multitask and prioritize, good mental and physical health, and an ability to talk your way out of trouble.

Most of these traits are pretty basic—again, simple but not easy. But when push comes to shove, they are easier said than done.

Let's look at "goal-oriented" as an example.

This trait can help a C/O through plenty of hard times, if she possesses it. It can sustain her after a grueling work day in the office when she's faced with even more late night street hours at her fifth operational meeting in a week, pretending to love and respect another despicable agent.

And while she's operating on that street, she's got

plenty more to deal with—from actual dangers to simple nuisances that could harm her, her agent, and/or make the whole operation more complicated—including potential terrorist and criminal attacks, roadside bombs, breakdowns, beggars, animals, awful roads, protests, agents who've gone bad, or just a friendly neighborhood hostile surveillance team out to catch her in the act and arrest her agent.

Add to this the stress of being away from family for months or even years, and the difficulties only compound. When it comes down to it, most people do not possess an Agency load of the seemingly simple quality of being goal-oriented.

Different traits are important when developing and recruiting an asset. Here the skill set seems murkier since there is debate about which approach works best—should you be the back-slapping, used car salesman who hunts his prey? Or the strong, silent type who lets potential targets come to him?

As usual, the answer is "it depends." It depends on the situation, the person you're going after, his country and culture. But the bottom line is, a good recruiter must play multiple roles: friend, mentor, protégé, therapist, barman, bagman, caseworker, cheerleader, humanitarian—and in times past, even pimp.

Perhaps most important for developmental operations, an officer needs to possess a quality that rarely shows its face these days: a personality. Just about any will do, even if it's not his own. Don't get me wrong. I'm not talking about displaying a phony personality. Most people can spot that from a mile away—but instead, faking the interest, turning on the charm, and upping the energy level.

In fact, acting plays a big role in being a successful Case Officer. When a meeting starts, a metaphorical camera goes on, a figurative director yells, "Action!"—and you're on. This is where C/Os really earn their pay. At this point, they must lean forward and pretend to be fascinated by even the most boring schmuck on the planet.

Acting's cousin, improvisation, is an equally important skill. Because C/Os never know what the other person may say or do at any moment, they must be able to adapt and react quickly.

Sadly, many C/Os don't possess much of a personality, real or fake. I found this most apparent in the younger C/Os who typically preferred the virtual to the real world, choosing their phones and screens over interacting with actual human beings.

But even though it's a relatively simple job, most C/Os, frankly, are not very good at it. A plethora of reasons could explain why—from a lack of education, language ability, sophistication, and/or international experience to simple laziness.

Comical examples of C/O clumsiness abound overseas. For instance, once a C/O picked up an asset in his car. It was a cold turnover, meaning that the previous handler was not at the meeting, and neither the new C/O nor the agent had ever met. The C/O drove to the location where the agent was supposed to wait, glanced around, and picked up a guy who fit his description. Unfortunately, he did away with any sort of tradecraft which would have ensured he found his man. The C/O told the asset he was glad to meet him, asked how much time he had, and said he was going to drive to the next town where they would talk. After a few questions about his work, however, it became abundantly clear that the man in his car was not the agent. He was simply a poor local who needed a lift and saw an opportunity in a friendly American with a shiny SUV.

Then, there is the unique experience of having grown up American. American culture teaches us to believe in fair play, that we should not take advantage of another's disadvantages. This implies that relationships should be above-board, transparent—even just—leading some young officers to question the rightness of using others to benefit the US government. After all, they've been taught that we're all one big global community, with the added American mandate to help the less-fortunate—in every country, not merely their own.

This mentality, however, is antithetical to espionage, to the essence of what a C/O does on a daily basis—and, frankly, to how most other countries and their people operate. Espionage can be a dirty, dangerous, and ugly business. Make no mistake—CIA-agent relationships are voluntary, but a C/O must still bribe, corrupt, manipulate, and prey on individuals and their vulnerabilities to get what she wants. Such relationships become a game of *quid pro quo*—if you help me out, maybe I'll return the favor.

Most Americans are not accustomed to that kind of life. American culture teaches the Calvinist principle that people simply get what they deserve, due to talent, hard work, and a system of just laws. But Calvinist America isn't the world of espionage.

Similarly, many C/Os grew up in middle-class households, from which they rarely witnessed how the other half lives. Their personal bubble included few international experiences or exposure to the rest of the world.

Many hadn't dealt with foreigners on a regular basis, let alone had meaningful relationships with them. As a result, they don't understand what they value or how often-precarious conditions affect the ways they think and act. As previously noted, officers also receive little formal instruction on the history, politics, or culture of their countries before going PCS.

In short, Case Officers fundamentally do not understand the foreigners they're assigned to work against.

These real-world experiences are important because so much of the C/O job description is unwritten. Problems arise with no textbook answers and which cannot be taught in any training class. In an ideal world, candidates would encounter some of these situations before applying to the Agency, learning lessons—often the hard way—from interacting with strangers in strange lands. Sadly, that's rarely the case.

Even sadder is the fact that many C/Os remain ignorant to such situations, even after working overseas. Ironically, this is especially true of those serving in the Third World, where they're typically far removed from the locals. In such countries, they often live, work, play, shop, eat, and drink in artificial bubbles of security.

The practice of intelligence becomes even stranger with the realization that finding new sources is often totally random. That's right—the entire foundation of human intelligence collection is largely based on chance. As in other relationships, many intelligence successes are pure luck, based upon who stumbles across your path on a given day, or who happens to walk in to station and volunteer.

And how often can you reliably expect really good,

even life-saving, sources to fall in your lap? Sometimes, perhaps. But really not that often.

So what's the result of feckless agents, low-skilled C/Os, and an overriding emphasis on quantity over quality? No surprise. Bad intelligence.

Many, maybe most, intelligence reports are wrong. The events they predict rarely pan out. For example, I reported on literally hundreds and hundreds of planned terrorist attacks in my career. Not a single one ever happened.

I'm happy about this, of course. But such outcomes also indicate the sources' lack of credibility.

In all fairness, the bar for reporting this type of threat intelligence is far lower since the Agency has a duty to warn and disseminate any potential threats—ironically, even to our sworn enemies, unless, of course, that threat comes from us.

But here's the real kicker—and why we don't stress too much about these problems. Most consumers of the reported information—the Intelligence Community, military, policymakers—already know these shortcomings. So most of the time, they don't bother to read the reports either, let alone, put them to some kind of practical use. Foreign policy decisions are generally not based on intelligence, assessments, or any kind of professional analysis. Threat information may be the only exception to this, but that's largely for CYA-related reasons, meaning that one must take precautions in the slim chance the report is true.

Instead, US foreign policy, especially big-ticket items, usually follows political platforms, what US government officials want to accomplish, and how they personally see the world, similar to how news outlets pick stories that fit their narratives. Both act like a scientist publishing a theory before performing the research. Decision-makers form opinions and choose their policies long before they receive classified briefings about what's actually going on in the world. Lower-level decisions are often made by government bureaucrats who don't like the Agency and therefore distrust its reporting.

For the record, I'm not picking on any particular administration (or news outlet). They all do it. Their campaigns hinge on various promises, and once in office, they're desperate to prove their rightness.

Human intelligence collection has become a giant, automated machine that spins day and night, costs billions of dollars, and risks thousands of lives, all to spit out stupendous numbers of reports that are often wrong and usually ignored—and which have only minimal effect when it comes to keeping America safe or promoting our interests abroad.

As a result, agents (and as we shall see in the next lesson, many C/Os) are largely expendable. It doesn't matter how much time, money, and risk were invested into recruiting them. They will be quickly let go for the most trivial reasons, all to clear the decks to hire new inconsequential bodies.

And yet, despite its flaws, our system is actually the best one out there.

Most intelligence services exist in name only. In reality, only a small handful, including the US, UK, France, Russia, and China, do any real work. Even those we are taught to fear—such as the Russians and Chinese—can be comically amateurish. Other services simply compile what a friendly country passed to them via an official exchange. Some even send their home office "intelligence" read in a local newspaper and disguised as an official report.

When it comes to developing countries, intelligence services exist primarily to sustain the corrupt regime upon which they are built. As a result, they excel at monitoring their own citizens, domestic communications, and opposition figures, but that's about it. They have few priorities (or capabilities) outside the country.

In America, our current intelligence priorities reflect those of our country—an interminable obsession with eliminating every risk in the big, scary world by throwing massive resources at potential threats and demonstrating our progress through often-meaningless numbers and statistics. In reality, one simply cannot cover, control, or regulate every dangerous aspect of life, and attempts to do so often cause more harm than good.

Obviously, C/Os are to blame for many weaknesses in the collection process. But then again, so is a system which not only hires unfit applicants, but ignores their bad behavior once on board.

Lesson Eight

C/Os as Agents

At a going-away party for a COS in the Caribbean, a senior US Navy officer spoke to the crowd about his departing friend, whom he contrasted favorably with his opinion of his friend's employer: "Until I met him, I never trusted the CIA," he said. "Most of those guys are just a bunch of bone-headed idiots who'll only let you down."

Clearly, the Navy officer had a chip on his shoulder. He didn't hesitate to express his true feelings, despite the fact that half the audience were station officers.

Still, I wasn't particularly surprised.

The CIA's relationship with the military is strained at best. The Defense Department's own intelligence agency, the DIA, refers to DO counterparts as "Klingons." Other military officials refer to Agency HQS as "The Death Star," and special operations officers call C/Os "The Pink Squad," laughing about how we supposedly hover far behind the front lines. Though ironically, even after saying such things, some then whisper that they'd love to join the organization.

But when it comes right down to it, the CIA doesn't play well with many parts of government.

A more colorful name used to describe its officers is a different take on the acronym: "Clowns In Action." This jab seems to have originated outside the Agency, but is muttered by its own employees these days. A newly hired desk officer even signed internal emails with the epithet.

I first heard it from a boss in the Middle East after I'd reminded him that I hadn't been paid by HQS in four months—not a penny. At that point, even I couldn't argue the jibe.

But it wasn't supposed to be this way.

The Agency claims to hire hard-working, upstanding patriots with character and integrity.

They must, the argument goes, since they do important work, often alone and without supervision. Thus, CIA personnel must have impeccable moral fiber. But these are largely specious, feel-good statements for employment ads and government oversight committees.

Indeed, the Agency may represent ideal qualities, but, in reality, rarely do such employees get hired. Most C/Os are far more mortal.

They're not just not superheroes. They're almost the complete opposite—a kind of anti-hero, with uncommon characteristics that make them do uncommon things.

Sound familiar?

That's right—like begets like. Antihero C/Os recruit antiheroes themselves—agents with just enough wretched qualities to be willing to commit espionage.

In fact, many C/Os sport the same attributes as their very own agents, enough to be considered distant relatives—or at the very least, agents-in-law.

To me, an organization which declares the search for truth to be its rallying cry should be different. It should be held to higher standards, with employees that soar above petty human weaknesses and predictability.

But as it turns out, it's nearly impossible to find such people—saints willing to commit sins, that is.

Yet perhaps this analysis isn't the whole story. After all, the CIA receives astronomical numbers of applications for a miniscule number of positions. They can afford to be picky.

Something bigger, perhaps murkier, may be at play.

Despite the conspiracy theory bells I just set to clanging, stay with me on this one. In my observation, the Agency is perfectly aware of the qualities their employees possess. So bringing sub-par candidates on board could very well be part of a diabolical—and ironic—plan.

The CIA recruits officers cut from the same cloth as those whom the officers will themselves recruit. And not just because they will, in this way, know their future targets well—after all, they'd just have to look in the mirror.

But keep in mind that an agent is a deeply flawed character—what kind of person agrees to betray his country? Agents encompass a mess of personal problems, defects, weaknesses. The DO calls these "motivations" and "vulnerabilities," with *delightful* tendencies like greed, addiction, marital problems, and hatred for leadership topping the list—though, these days, some officers actually frown on working with assets who possess such qualities.

In other words, the more complicated and flawed the person, the better the agent—or, at least, the easier to recruit and retain him. Why? Because each of these tendencies can be exploited for a larger purpose.

The CIA recognizes the power of such traits even within its own workforce.

Hence, Case Officers should possess qualities that

make them do things ordinary people refuse. Things like taking rigorous and uncomfortable polygraph tests; waiting months and years to hear whether they got a job; devoting huge chunks of their lives to far-off, absurd places few have even heard of; enduring rules and regulations that restrict personal freedom and define their lifestyles; remaining silent about what they do for a living; receiving little praise or glory for accomplishments; putting their lives in danger; and enduring daily hardships, often away from family, friends, and the comfortable trappings of home.

In this vein, an ideal C/O's motivations should include love of money, love of country, desire for job security, and a need to feel special. And as for closely related vulnerabilities—insecurity, inferiority, laziness, marital problems, a need for attention, and/or a desire to feel powerful and important would work just fine.

Want proof?

During an operation, an Agency surveillance team was setting up on a target at the ideal observation point, located in a nearby café. One of the officers, however, refused to use the location because the café required patrons to order food or drinks, and he didn't want to spend a cent of his *per diem* overseas. He fought so hard, the team set up in a park further away that saved him a couple bucks but didn't provide the same visibility.

There are heaps of ridiculous examples of Scrooge C/Os who loved money enough to hoard every penny of their daily allowance while on Temporary Duty, or TDY. One C/O took beef bouillon cubes from the station's supply to his hotel, turned them into a rudimentary soup, and slurped the whole thing down every night to avoid eating out. Another filled a suitcase with cans of tuna fish before departing to avoid spending money in local restaurants.

In East Africa, an older married couple—already very well-off—stayed in the cheapest hotel they could find during a three-month TDY in order to pocket the maximum amount of their *per diem* and buy a car when they returned. The result of their little experiment? They were miserable the entire trip and took their frustrations out on each other and everyone in the office. Here's hoping a new Prius was worth it.

Others can't do without their personal comforts. One insisted on drinking Pepsi in a country full of Coke, bringing along cases of the stuff.

Personnel officers revealed that C/Os complain to them about—literally—being underpaid by a nickel or dime in their paychecks.

Others' marital problems lead them to cheat on their spouses during their TDYs, removing their rings after take-off and redefining the TDY acronym to mean "Temporarily Divorced."

The same qualities exist at HQS. There, a few small shops sell candy, gum, and sandwiches. A shop located in the basement was nicknamed the "Blind-Man's Stand" because it was run—you guessed it—by a blind man. Yet instead of supporting an entrepreneur who clearly faced challenges, a few employees used his disability against him—cheating him by handing him paper bills they claimed were larger than they actually were.

Laziness, too, abounds at the Agency. While some officers accomplish a lot—laboring away even in hardship locations—they're the minority. Too many C/Os fritter away their time in cushy, overseas assignments. And at HQS, the situation can be even worse. Many employees are just bureaucratic clock-watchers—readying themselves all day for the five o'clock stampede.

Even C/Os recognize the similarities between ourselves and our targets. When a C/O was unexpectedly pitched by an opposition service—if, for example, a Russian officer attempted to recruit him—we used to ask the C/O which vulnerabilities he'd displayed to make the Russian think he could hire him. We were joking, of course, except that we weren't.

In the end, while C/Os are supposed to set themselves apart from their agents, many actually reflect them instead.

Why? Because we're all playing the same game.

C/Os handle agents. They vet, hire, train, and task them to do what they want. The agents report information back to their handlers. In return, they receive a salary and some perks, and let's face it—most agents are in it for the money.

HQS handles C/Os. It vets, hires, trains, and tasks them to do what it wants. C/Os report information back to their HQS handlers via cables. In return, they receive a salary and some perks, and let's face it—most C/Os are also in it for the cash.

The DO runs on the puppet master principle. C/Os control agents and are, in turn, controlled by HQS. So not only does the Agency hire people with undesirable qualities, they nurture and encourage such qualities once they're in place.

Insecurity is perhaps the most popular flaw. The more angst and anxiety—the better. Why? Because insecure officers feel like they have something to prove. They're shells without the money, the prestige, the identity. So they'll endure more hardships, and even more absurdities to maintain their status.

I could tell almost immediately when I met a fellow Case Officer. They gave off this strange vibe of both insecurity and arrogance—perhaps because such qualities naturally go hand in hand. And forget about a real conversation. Any attempt became a monologue on his part. If I said something amusing, she'd try to one-up me. Showing any real interest or empathy only diminished their weak control over their own prominence.

Just being around some of them hurt my soul. Unless, of course, they wanted something from me. Then, they could turn on the charm like nobody's business.

In my sad experience, this only worsened with age. Hanging out in the same room with a bunch of old, retired C/Os is a unique experience, as each tries to outdo the other with his war stories. While everyone talks, no one seems to listen.

Perhaps not surprisingly, then, most C/Os end up loners, insecure or not. After all, saving the world is a solitary business.

Espionage is not a team sport—one of many misconceptions. There *is* an "I" in station. So C/Os work alone, and the mythical reality of a secret brotherhood within the CIA is just that—a myth.

The CIA is not one big, happy family.

Rather, it's every spy for himself. There's little comradery or *esprit de corps*. Each C/O is an Army of One—or an Agency of One, in this case. This means no one's looking out for anyone—other than himself. Instead, they're punching the time card to collect more money and benefits, more praise and attention, with the hopes of reaching their twenty-year retirement date in one piece.

Within the office, C/Os work individually, writing up the results of meetings from the day before or prepping for the night to come. In stark contrast to rooms of personnel dictating each Hollywood case, real-world cases, whether developmental or recruited, are a one-man show. Whatever they do or don't accomplish will be a direct result of a single C/O's skills, smarts, and creativity.

Given their choice of colleagues, most C/Os prefer it this way.

That doesn't stop HQS from periodically attempting to join different directorates together, such as C/Os and analysts, AKA the Directorate of Operations with the Directorate of Intelligence, or DI. But there is a potent "us vs. them" mentality among differing professions within the organization—in fact, C/Os refer to analysts as "DI weenies" all the time. Thus, such initiatives don't tend to work well, as each side resists singing Kumbaya as long as possible.

C/Os are simply competitors. On paper, they're in this thing together, but they play like opposing quarterbacks, making for a strange office dynamic that demands feigned comradery amidst intense competition to find the best targets, recruit the most sources, and produce the highest number of reports.

The sad result is that no one feels the slightest joy if another C/O pulls off a great operation. Their success only makes the rest of the station look worse—and their jobs that much harder. Indeed, there is no sadder moment than when a colleague gets promoted.

This dynamic, fed by personal insecurities, is

encouraged by the Agency. As in a cage match, the competition can bring out the best in a fighter. It's what gets him out of bed early in the morning and keeps him on the street until late at night. It's what drives her to schedule yet another developmental meeting with that painful Chinese Second Secretary—the plump one who burps, picks his teeth, and eats with his mouth wide-open.

So the insecurity goes round and round, feeding on itself in one enormous, infinite loop—while strangely forming part of the bedrock of the great US national security system.

The CIA claims the opposite, of course. They insist that we're all one team, pulling together to get the big win.

I admit, the mixed messages confused me in the beginning. Back then, I wished we were on the same team, that we all worked together and had each other's backs. Before I joined, I yearned for that part of the job. But I could not have been more wrong. Don't join the Agency for brotherhood. If that's what you're searching for, the military's your game. But if you're a loner, try your hand at the CIA.

Long story short? If you liked high school, you'll love the Agency. Just think of the fun you'll have in staff meetings.

So as a C/O exploits an agent's vulnerabilities, the CIA also exploits the neediness of its officers to reinforce control.

To paraphrase a manager who described his ideal subordinate: I don't want some adventurous, freethinking C/O working for me. I want a guy with a family and a mortgage he has to pay each month. That way, I know he'll show up to work on time and do what I tell him.

In other words, the Agency operates on the assumption that its employees are driven by the lowest common denominators—that, for the most part, they exist without any internal mechanism for honesty, loyalty, and hard work. So they groom officers as codependents, with sufficient motivations to keep them attached to the organization, but not so many as to spoil them.

This system creates a delicately balanced, bizarrely optimal level of dysfunction. The ideal is a broken but still working officer—a "functioning alcoholic," so to speak. It can all go horribly wrong if the person tips too far to one side.

In sum, maybe there is an "art" or "craft" to intelligence. But the players in this game don't usually match such lofty language, no matter what the newest spy kiss-and-tell proclaims. Those post-CIA wannabe celebrities are using the same tactics to recruit their readers as they did their agents.

Lesson Nine

What Do Spies and Lovers Have in Common?

If espionage were a romantic affair, the recruitment cycle would be the search for Mr. (or Mrs.) Right.

Just like any relationship, recruitment takes officers on a rollercoaster of emotions—from self-doubt and fear of rejection, to the excitement of the chase, and finally, to the joy of requited feelings.

Such a relationship is built on trust and honesty, as so much of it is dirty and forbidden—leading to a climax that may be a conquest or a brief coming together—an almost-happy ending, if not a happily-ever-after.

Within the narrative of espionage, the words spy and lover are interchangeable.

First, a human being needs companionship. Similarly, a C/O, according to her job description, must find new sources to prove her worth and competence—even her allure.

So a C/O goes out to spot someone. He hangs out at public places, receptions and parties, bars and restaurants, searching for the perfect mate. When a target sits beside him on a bus or airplane, it's a happy coincidence—Fate must be smiling upon him.

At other times, he meets potential agents through friends nice enough to set him up.

A C/O may even bump into an attractive person at the supermarket. She makes it seem like an accident, of course, like she'd never been following him, had never noticed the official government license plate in the parking lot identifying him as a target of interest.

As previously discussed, some truly desperate C/Os are content to settle with Mr. Right-*Now*—the lowest-hanging fruit on the vine. While he may not meet all of their requirements, he's available immediately, so they'll go ahead and swallow their pride to pick him up. Indeed, some such conquests are so available, they'll actually walk in and volunteer their services without any effort required on your part.

Of course, just like serial lovers, some C/Os are better than others in the early innings of the game. You know the type that can walk into almost any place and pick up whomever they like. Others lack such confidence, however, and end up alone for most of the evening.

But for virtually everyone, the first step is to make a good impression. That means dressing nicely, acting friendly and polite, and showing that we're professional—and discreet. After all, this could become a long-term, sensitive relationship. Both the target and the C/O need to know that lips will be sealed, that no wife, friends, or colleagues will get an earful. After all, getting caught could mean serious trouble all around.

So the next goal is to get the target to like and trust us enough to meet again. And just like any forbidden relationship, future encounters should take place somewhere private, one-on-one, where both parties can speak candidly and get to know each other—far away from any prying eyes.

But that's the ideal scenario. Even among the best of the players, many targets won't agree to a second meeting. Some will be suspicious of a C/O's true intentions, afraid that he's only interested in their body . . . of information. That means thick skin is a must in this game. Because one thing is for certain: with or without a wingman, C/Os are repeatedly shot down, no matter how smooth.

But if he does agree, then it's time to assess him—to feel him out, see what he's like, find out if there's more than just a surface-level attraction. A few meetings should satisfy questions about his background, whether he's trustworthy, whether he's really worth investing in.

You will also find out if he wants to continue seeing you. After all, as in any relationship, it takes two to tango.

And once they're both on the dance floor, it's time for the C/O to begin to develop her prospective mate—to turn a person into a case and then into an agent. She wines and dines him, takes him hiking and golfing, shows him a good time, and builds that all-important rapport. She will always pick up the tab. In fact, she insists on paying, thereby proving that she's not only capable of taking good care of him, but that she's also in the driver's seat.

This developmental phase requires months, even years. All the while, the C/O is getting to know his target, his likes and dislikes, personal problems, professional responsibilities, hopes and dreams. He learns about his attractive qualities, determines whether he's suitable for this kind of relationship. He smokes out any skeletons in the closet—counterintelligence or security issues that could signal trouble for him or the Agency. And he validates—though, as we've already seen, usually not as much as he should.

This is the stage when the C/O determines whether the affair could, in fact, go all the way. She drops hints about her likes and dislikes. She tells him what she wants from him, watches to see if he'll follow directions. If she's lucky, he may even give sneak peeks of what to expect further down the line, talking dirty with shared tidbits of intimate information, proving that he's interested in being more than just friends. That's when her heart will start pumping. To protect him, she'll devise ostensible reasons to explain why they're together, doing her part to cover up the illicit affair.

At this point, things are getting exciting, but any good C/O knows he can't give into the temptation to consummate the relationship just yet. He has to stay the course, follow official protocol, convince those in charge that he and his developmental are meant to be together—because only truly experienced, senior-level officers get free rein to go all the way at such an early stage—that is, to pitch someone without asking formal permission.

That means every C/O must plead their case, sift all the information into categories like background, access, motivations, vulnerabilities—prove that he is, indeed, marriage material and worth bringing into the family.

Eventually, the magical day comes when she's ready to seal the deal. The developmental has proven his desire for a real, long-term relationship by meeting secretly, accepting money, and trusting her with sensitive information that, if found out, would get him into heaps of trouble. Just as important, she now has that official permission from the Agency to pop the question.

It's time to bring him to some discreet location late at night to take the friendship to the next level—to tie the knot, make the whole thing official—if not in the eyes of the church, then at least in those of a secular institution.

It's time to recruit a CIA agent.

If the developmental phase was done right, the recruitment pitch shouldn't be much of a surprise. After all, he's no idiot. Any target worth their salt has known for some time that the CIA was interested in him—perhaps it was even love at first sight. He's been cheating on others around him—telling secrets about his employer and lying to his family about his whereabouts, risking everything for this chance.

So his response, too, shouldn't be much of a surprise. A good C/O knows his answer before popping the question—or he's at least pretty sure. The Agency doesn't provide concurrence to recruit unless it's confident of success. It hates surprises.

When a recruit says "yes," he'll become a partner or private consultant, at least on the surface. A C/O may even refer to him in such ways as to make him feel equal in the relationship.

He agrees to receive a salary in exchange for providing protected information, helping to safeguard the meetings, and keeping the relationship secret. After all, he's no longer just a friend. Much has changed, now that it's official.

It's a strange relationship, in truth, more like prostitution than matrimony—my, how the oldest profession resembles the second-oldest.

Once he's on the payroll, he's technically a pro. That

means the "romance" is all but snuffed out by business, establishing a professional routine that gets the job done—meeting in private—often a car or hotel room—doing business, making payment, and slipping out the back door. Good-bye, restaurants and flowers and mints on the pillow. Hello, clean and loveless relationship—with a periodic gift—maybe a bonus or some booze—just to remind him he's special.

Despite the drawbacks, it's a more efficient and secure relationship. There's no need to dance around the truth anymore. When a C/O and agent fully understand each other, each can be more direct. So as with any pro, you tell him exactly what you like and want, and he tries to give it to you—at least, better than any normal partner would.

In some ways, little has changed. Indeed, a real pro and a good C/O are skilled at faking it—making each other believe they are truly special, that they're only doing what they're doing because they like the other.

But as in any business relationship, neither side personally cares much for the other. Everyone's in it for their own selfish reasons and knows it will end whenever they become obsolete. After all, it's just business.

At the same time, the relationship is meant to be a committed one, pledged with a signature on a document claiming that he will remain faithful and keep the relationship under wraps. In truth, he does so largely because it's in his best interest.

But no matter how wet the ink on the dotted line, his eye may still wander. He may even cheat with another exotic—and rich—foreigner willing to shower him with the same attention—and money—in exchange for the goods he has to offer. Some promiscuous agents juggle multiple affairs at the same time, while successfully keeping them secret from each other. So validation continues to play an important part in the relationship—even well after recruitment.

But in the end, all love fades. C/Os and agents may fall out of love because an agent loses the access that made him attractive in the first place. He may drop out because he's not being "appreciated" enough financially, or because he sees the whole thing as just too risky.

It's now time to terminate that agent.

Whatever the reason for the break-up, it's never easy to drop this news on the other person. Not after all you've been through together.

Still, it's probably for the best—and it's all part of the natural (recruitment) cycle of life, fraught with its own platitudes and clichés: you'll always care for him; it's not you, it's me; your interests and priorities have changed; you're leaving town and simply can't see him anymore.

C/Os are even authorized to give a little money at parting—a kind of alimony, so to speak—to help ease the pain and transition. That, and you never know, he might prove useful in the future and up for re-recruiting.

But the fact remains that a termination bonus is primarily insurance against a bad breakup—so he won't go away mad but will just go away. Nobody wants a former agent running into the arms of someone else, spilling his guts about all you did together, or taking a baseball bat to his C/O's car.

In the end, C/Os rarely remember their agents anyway. Once the ties are severed, they've moved on, met someone else, begun plotting a new relationship. Promotions don't come easy, after all, and in this game, the best players always win.

Lesson Ten

A Closed System

Let's go back to anthropology class for a moment.

The CIA operates a covert training base in the South, its perimeter protected by a high metal fence. Deer living on base are trapped inside, unable to leave or bring new animals into the herd.

As a result, those deer have been inbreeding for years, leading to various strange diseases and physical defects among the population.

In anthropology, we learn to view society as a system composed of variables, including economy, ideology, and social structure. Change in the system can occur when said variables come into contact with influences from the outside.

The Agency is largely a closed system due to the nature of its work. Fewer external influences are allowed to enter.

This closed system affects its animals—and its humans. Demeanors often become distorted and confused as a result of their suffocation from the outside world. Even seasoned officers crumble beneath the soul-crushing bureaucracy, ultimately resembling—at least psychologically—the deformed deer on base.

Of course, no system is entirely closed. Even North

Korea trades with its neighbors and welcomes the occasional tourist.

The CIA is no different. While ostensibly sealed by walls and fences, CIA installations have gates in and out, allowing some of the outside world to seep in from time to time. Employees come and go, bringing with them ideas from their everyday lives, some of which have been integrated into the culture, though perhaps at a slower rate than other institutions. The organization cannot entirely escape reflecting society.

Such influences exist in the real world. Supervisors complain that the new generation doesn't like to be told what to do, needs constant feedback on their performance, and prioritizes lifestyle over work, leaving all-too-early every day. In my particular case, the younger generation's notorious aversion to making eye contact only made me stare more.

Within the current CIA, younger personnel are also not especially loyal. They refuse to be tied down to any one organization—no matter what the organization—for too long. In fact, so many have left the DO after only brief stints that newly hired C/Os are now required to sign contracts guaranteeing that they will stay put for at least five years.

Other examples are more absurd. A senior officer shared that she'd been emailed by her youthful colleagues—even though they sat beside her in their cubicles. She reacted by standing up and answering their questions out loud, earning herself a complaint and a visit from the boss, who admonished the officer to only respond via the computer.

By the way, these events happened not in some safe space in a domestic office, but half-way across the globe at a rough and tumble station in West Africa, where you might expect the personnel to be a little tougher.

The current American obsession with security has also penetrated the Agency, manifesting itself in two ways.

First, the organization is even more consumed with hiring squeaky-clean applicants who look safe and accomplished—at least on paper.

In fact, a former CIA Director, who worked briefly as a C/O early in his career, famously admitted that even he would have difficulty getting into the organization these days, based on the qualifications of most applicants.

These hyper-competitive resumes are important documents—if a skeleton emerges from a C/O's future closet, his recruitment officer can justify why she brought him on board. As a result, CYA plays a significant role even in hiring decisions.

But such credentials are often just for show. While they ooze quantity, they contain few meaningful experiences. Just scratch and sniff, and you'll find the same applicants as before, only now their resumes have been stuffed with even more bullet points.

Second, the obsession with security affects Agency operations. Today, an officer's fear of upsetting the *status quo* can be overwhelming. The name of the game for the CIA, like the rest of the country, is preservation of resources. Operationally, this means not falling back, but it also means not moving forward—and therefore holding still. What kind of personnel sticks their neck out in that kind of environment?

Despite the fact that some of the outside world slips into the Agency, relatively little of its insides find their way out. In other words, very few details about its people or products are revealed to others.

This is perfectly fine as long as everyone's doing the right thing. But the rotten sides of human nature remind us over and over again that they're often not. The Agency, as a closed system made up of human beings, desperately needs an outsider to check its math from time to time.

The all-powerful Office of Personnel Security is assigned this task from the inside, but who watches over them? Their work is so super-secret, the office exists as a closed system within another closed system. So what they actually do can't be seen, let alone challenged, by almost anyone. And if the quality of work exhibited by other Agency personnel is any indicator, chances are there's plenty worth challenging.

Bodies outside the organization—but still within the government—also enjoy mighty oversight authority. In fact, Congress is one of the last bastions to guarantee honesty within the system. And while it actually has the right to look under the Agency's hood, its members serve primarily as cogs in the same machine, rather than objective watchdogs. So this part of the equation has turned into the blind leading—or, in this case, watching over—the blind.

How so?

First of all, most legislative officials have little or no background in intelligence, leading to fundamental misunderstandings of the business they've been charged to regulate. In this vein, officials are afraid of interfering too much, so they're prone to accept virtually any explanations the CIA provides. Like the rest of the country, their impressions about the Agency largely come from popular culture. This mentality exhibits itself in their feedback on briefings about current operations. And stations are happy to perpetuate their ignorance, revealing only the barest facts so that congressional visitors will ask few follow-up questions and quickly lose interest.

Let's not forget that these watchdogs are also elected officials whose main objective is to get *re*-elected. So like the rest of the Agency, they're also interested in preserving the *status quo*. As I mentioned before, all cogs in the same machine. So they're not especially eager to check under stray rocks or throw monkey wrenches into Agency operations.

Even those politicians who do publicly criticize the Agency privately apologize to officers when the cameras are off, admitting the bravado was for the benefit of their constituencies.

Congress relies on the honesty of DO officers—and in all honesty, most C/Os would never risk their careers by implicating themselves or their employer. These officers fear that such revelations would lead other Agency officers to conclude they'd been betrayed to an outsider. Thus, unless genuinely disgruntled, DO loyalty forever lies with the Agency.

In line with this loyalty, there exists a tribal-like pressure for C/Os to keep outsiders from interfering in Agency business. This pressure justifies officers in keeping their cards—and mistakes—close to the vest. "Others just don't understand," they reason among themselves. And as for strangers who attempt to challenge the CIA's work? They're messing with a higher purpose.

As a COS in Africa warned his station personnel on the eve of an important congressional delegation: "Remember. No matter what they ask, we don't discuss our problems with others—even official delegations. We handle them internally."

The news media also monitors the Agency. But like legislators, journalists are also stuck between a rock and a hard place. Assigned to report on a secret organization, they must wholly rely on officially approved information since using confidential sources inside the organization can be illegal.

The effects of a closed system are especially glaring in the media. Unique insights about the organization—or for that matter, the most sensitive national security matters—are usually based on rumor and speculation. I was fortunate enough to be involved in high-profile issues that received news coverage. Much of the reporting to the public was simply wrong—and sometimes comically so.

Without access to sensitive information, the media seeks to undermine the CIA under the label of "investigative journalism"—including publishing locations of secret installations in the US and overseas. When I see such pieces, I ask myself whether these so-called journalists are serving the American cause, whether their work is supposed to benefit the greater good of the country. If I can answer "yes" to both questions, how in the world would publishing such revelations do anything other than endanger the people who work at the outed installations?

At other times, the media will publish whatever it can get. In these cases, the bar is so low that virtually anything will do. A few years back, breaking news erupted in a DC paper—the CIA had finally allowed its employees to bring their own mini-fridges into HQS. *What a scoop!*

So as a closed system, the CIA is generally off-limits to the outside world. While necessary, such restrictions lead to unintended consequences. As a rule, closed systems are rarely healthy, breeding suspicion of outside influences and resisting change. The Agency's conservative culture is all the more striking, given the rapid pace of change in the rest of the world.

Ironically, books like this one are some of the few approved sources of information about the Agency. Without them, how would anyone actually know what really happens inside—and how would anything ever change?

On the other hand, I wonder if this is as good as it gets at the CIA. Maybe its glory days are in the past and the future—or maybe, just in our imagination. Maybe the organization is like any other variable in society—education, culture, politics—serving as a simple reflection of the times in which we find ourselves. After all, every country goes through cycles and mood swings based on internal and external events.

And let's face it. We seem to be at a low point in history—been that way since the end of the Cold War, when the Agency was at its apex. Countries, like people, need struggles to become great. Otherwise, all they'll end up striving for is personal safety and comfort. That description seems appropriate for a retirement community, not a great country or intelligence service.

Still, I refuse to believe there isn't room to grow, to adapt, to become better. Ultimately, human intelligence remains a human business, and the CIA will win or lose because of its people, the one variable they can still control. Perhaps the path to ultimate renewal simply means following the old cliché that's been recommended for years: hire, train, and retain the best people you can find.

Lesson Eleven

Why the Good Ones Leave

I enjoyed walking down a certain hallway close to the main entrance at HQS. Every few months, a conference room hosted CIA 101, a two-week introductory course for new employees. The latest batch of dewy-eyed, would-be Case Officers spilled out into that hallway at break time, testosterone bubbling in every last one of them—women included.

Ah, the new recruits. Yet another ripe bunch of James and Joan Bonds hired to save the world. Each still believing the myths and legends, each ignorant of the systematic crushing of their hopes and dreams somewhere down the career path.

Because of its mission, the CIA still attracts a fair number of idealists, though they're increasingly the minority, representing maybe ten or twenty percent of new employees.

This eagerness lasts a few months or years. Then, inevitably, something happens—some setback, some eye-opening moment when that feels more like a systemic body-slam. That's when the testosterone starts to wear off, when the dream begins to fade. It's then that any remaining idealists realize the CIA's not what they thought after all.

I was one of those idealists, one of those who starts

off soaring and falls way too hard. Perhaps, I recognized the younger me in one of those officers who spilled out into that hallway.

We don't join for the money or the perks, but for more intangible reasons: to live up to our potential, perhaps fulfill a mission in life. We join to serve the country, sacrifice for the homeland, use our talents for some greater good—and perhaps taste a little action and adventure.

So when idealists like us learn that the Agency often doesn't complement these priorities, our whole world view, even our reason for being, is turned upside down.

Every idealist will ultimately come to a fork in the road, at which point she must choose whether to stick it out or flip a U-turn and rejoin the mortals on the outside.

Some of us suck it up and stay the course. But a surprising number leave.

The number of C/Os who resign from the CIA varies year by year, based in part on the health of the economy and the current wars in which the US is engaged. A few of my classmates left after their first tours, only to return after 9/11, motivated by the desire to join the fight. Even so, many classmates didn't make it to the magic twenty-year mark.

Joining the Agency is like getting married. Some go into the institution full of love and passion, with sky-high hopes and extraordinary expectations. These officers are ready to devote their entire lives to something bigger than themselves.

But as in a failed marriage, they wake up one day and realize that they don't know the one they fell in love with anymore. While they still care, the other doesn't feel the same way about them. Clearly, they loved too much, too deep, too hard—or simply, their expectations were out of whack.

Most who leave do so after completing their first or second tour, a typical decision point. By then, they've had plenty of time to analyze whether their disillusionment was temporary—perhaps the result of a bad tour or a lousy boss—or whether it emerged from systemic problems.

This lesson will, naturally, include a laundry list of the kinds of complaints a departing C/O would say at her exit interview, if there were such a thing. But as with most professions, the decision to leave usually comes down to disappointment—when an officer is discouraged enough by the reality of the job that she simply cannot carry on anymore, she gets out.

Which begs the question: Was her disappointment the result of runaway idealism or systemic failure?

Disappointment is, of course, the difference between expectations and reality.

Because most of the CIA's work is secret, popular culture replaces the unknown with—what else?—unrealistic but entertaining visions of the world of espionage. Add a healthy dose of myth, legend, and wish fulfillment, and shake well. Yours truly gulped large amounts of this potion.

Others base their sky-high expectations off actual history. Some believe they'll blow up bridges, sabotage trains, take out foreign leaders. The predecessor to the CIA, the OSS, actually did these things during WWII. But the OSS is long-gone, and real-life isn't an episode of *Hogan's Heroes*.

Such expectations share little in common with the modern Agency.

Time for that laundry list of Agency complaints, the realities that promise to shatter even the most-stubborn idealist.

While some grievances have already been discussed, including Agency emphasis on quantity over quality and scarcity of verifiable oversight, for me, the lack of deep, honest comradery finally cracked my idealistic armor. The DO resembles a random group of strangers staring at personal computers more closely than it does a tight-knit, dedicated team. And as previously noted, insecurity, competition, even animosity, are actually encouraged by the Agency.

I had joined for that special team, to take my place in a hallowed group with a higher purpose. But in this regard, I couldn't have been farther from the truth.

Not surprisingly, there's also little comradery within the US government as a whole. Relations between departments run hot and cold, giving rise to constant turmoil between the CIA, the military, and the State Department. Even these parts of government scarcely understand what the Agency really does, assuming its officers will do nothing but get in the way. Others think they know the CIA and simply consider its work stupid, actively trying to sabotage officers with loud, public games of "spot the spook."

C/Os used to be, for lack of a better word, the stars of the show—the beating heart of the CIA's mission and the reason for its existence. These days, however, they're just another job title in a massive bureaucracy.

The latest wave of militant egalitarianism teaches that everyone is the same—even at the Agency. Every single employee, from van driver all the way up to COS, is vitally important and considered equal. Though reality tells us nothing has changed, that the mission is just as hierarchical as ever, any kind of special treatment, whether or not it actually benefits the mission, is still frowned upon. Now, everyone is special—which means no one is.

In past years, operations also took precedence. All energy, focus, and attention funneled to the most important part of the mission, the pointy edge of the spear—the only reason to be in business.

In those days, the Mother Ship followed suit. HQS supported the Field—with a capital "F." Stations were largely autonomous units, granted freedom and responsibility to conduct their own operations, and every player in the game recognized where the real work happened. HQS assisted when needed, but otherwise, stayed the hell away.

That's all changed.

The field—with a small "f"—now serves and supports HQS. In today's world, the Mother Ship matters more than any station, and all power radiates from Washington. DC tasks the field and guides its mission. And because HQS is completely consumed with avoiding flaps that make it look bad, it demands time-consuming, box-checking updates from the field on the status of its operations.

Meanwhile, providing assistance is now an afterthought, as station requests go unanswered for extraordinary lengths of time. In fact, it's practically SOP that HQS won't respond until the third or fourth request from the field.

Paradoxically, despite the smallness of the world and the CIA's efforts to assert control over its personnel, the disconnect between HQS and the field has never been greater—ironic for an organization of supposed experts in collecting and communicating information. The Agency prides itself on understanding other countries and cultures, but it hardly knows (or seems to care) about its own people.

Part of this problem is cultural, since yet another "us vs. them" mentality exists—this time within the HQS/field dynamic. Because overseas officers work very different jobs than their HQS colleagues, they empathize very little with what happens back home, and vice versa.

This situation is humorously demonstrated when a C/O returns from the field. Previously, when HQS and the field disagreed, he sided with his station against the "nincompoops" in Washington. But because he's now back at HQS, he takes its side and blames the field for everything that goes wrong.

None of this is surprising. With the frequent personnel changes, there's almost no accountability at HQS. As a C/O in the field, you rarely know who—if anyone—you're dealing with on the other end of the line.

Thanks to HQS, station support staff isn't much help either. In some ways, these are the most powerful people at the Agency, capable of making each tour go easy or hard. In fact, when they arrive at a new station, C/Os are advised to "recruit" support staff—in other words, turn on the charm so they'll help out more readily.

If only it were that easy.

In a world turned upside down, support officers in the field are often too busy supporting HQS—or themselves—to get around to Case Officers. HQS levies so many of its own requirements, support officers are left with little time to take care of station matters. As a result, admin assistance at most stations is self-service at best. C/Os now spend far too much time just trying to get what they need to do their job.

CIA leadership has consented to such paradigm shifts due to fear of upsetting the rank-and-file workers who keep the lights on. That leadership continues to praise the hard work and dedication of the support staff despite the falsehoods inherent in those words.

In addition to a fear of confrontation, the CIA, like the US as a whole, has been struck in recent years by another dreadful disease: risk aversion. Symptoms include afflicting ordinary personnel with control-freak tendencies.

It used to be that sitting at your desk in the middle of the day only earned you slacker status, because you were expected to be out on the street ginning up new operations. In fact, a former boss once told the story of an infamous C/O who would actually disappear from station for weeks at a time—without telling a soul where he was going—and magically reappear with a stack of receipts and a pile of reports to submit.

These days, the opposite is true. Those who leave their desks are the slackers now, as the COS needs complete control and accountability to ensure that nothing goes wrong in his domain. That means operations—even within most stations—don't take priority anymore. Ironically, while glorifying that bygone era, that same former boss ensured that all of his C/Os dutifully sat at their desks during working hours in order to participate in *ad hoc* staff meetings. If a C/O went unaccounted for even one day, he would have been sent home.

So while Case Officer is still a unique position, it's become little more than an office job. C/Os sit most of the day at a desk, all dressed up, staring at a computer.

They breathe artificial air because windows can't be opened for security reasons—that is, of course, if they're lucky enough to work at a station with windows at all.

C/Os spend plenty of time playing office politics, worrying about how to say the right things, befriend the right people, and whether they've upset the wrong ones. In fact, I usually felt more stress and strain from dealing with my co-workers than I did from the work itself. When they're not playing politics, C/Os spend the remainder of their office time doing paperwork, writing reports, and sitting in staff meetings.

The problem is, espionage is largely an outdoor sport of chance and patience—not an indoor one packed with endless staff meetings. Officers in the field must be given extra-long leashes to explore leads, feel people out, and most of all, take some chances.

But in order to exercise their all-important control, the Agency continues to add more and more layers of meaningless bureaucracy that almost guarantee nothing significant will ever get done—more forms to complete, more boxes to check, more approvals to request. Authority and permission are disseminated among an even-greater number of managers to ensure that no single person can screw something up—or be blamed when something gets screwed up. Sometimes a dozen different people must sign off on a simple HQS cable.

Thus, CIA officials no longer seek operational outcomes. The process has become the purpose, so simply opera*ting* is now the opera*tion*.

In such an environment, the natural reaction of most employees is to shelter in place, stick to their desks, and keep their heads down—all while counting the days until retirement. And I really can't blame them for it. There's little to gain and everything to lose for acting out.

As a result, the CIA might as well be a giant treadmill. The ideal employee will walk briskly on the machine, appearing to the casual observer to work hard and move forward. But in reality, he simply stays in place, making no progress but also causing no disturbances.

Some climb the ranks by playing politics, which frankly isn't surprising. C/Os are reminded regularly to use their powers for good, not evil—in other words, to not "case-officer" each other, as they're all on the same team. But many do it anyway—and they've reached the tippy-top of the hierarchy.

One COS mastered a program of internal operations which catapulted him to the senior ranks.

First, he built allies by taking good care of those around him. He recommended them for promotions and handed out cash bonuses called Exceptional Performance Awards, or EPAs—whether they deserved them or not. In fact, the more mediocre an officer, the better, because those officers knew full-well that they owed their good fortune to the boss.

And he didn't just spoil his friends. He kept his enemies—particularly those who might slow his ascent—even closer by presenting them with well-timed EPAs, effectively killing them with kindness and confusing their plans and intentions. After all, how do you file a complaint against someone who just sent you a big chunk of money?

This COS especially enjoyed doling out bonuses to those at the end of their tours, so that, no matter how they felt about his leadership—which, other than his Machiavellian-level of paranoia, frankly wasn't that bad—they were more likely to leave with a smile if their pockets were stuffed with hush money.

He was also a pro when it came to telling the higher-ups what they wanted to hear—that is, that everything was perfectly fine in station, even when it wasn't. After all, HQS doesn't want controversies or problems. Putting out fires is merely annoying and time-consuming, accomplishing nothing but to make the organization look bad.

Obviously, gaming the system is a rather cynical and lazy strategy. But wannabe politicians like this COS have figured out what the Agency prioritizes these days—safety, security, clean operations, political correctness, surprise-free days—and they deliver. They say "no" much more than "yes"—it's far easier to do and often the first word out of their mouths. They take few chances, so little goes wrong—or, of course, right. But at the end of the day, that's what the Mother Ship wants.

Still, there are more benefits to being promoted than just more money. A C/O colleague had figured out that the quicker she rose to the top, the less likely anyone—including the all-powerful Office of Personnel Security—could mess with her. After all, poor results on a polygraph mean different things to an entry-level officer versus a member of the Senior Intelligence Service.

But while some get positions they don't deserve, the CIA as a whole is pretty fair in promoting its best officers, one of its more noble qualities. The Agency tends to recognize talent and dedication. So if you are smart, work hard, and take difficult assignments, you will likely go far. In fact, the organization has famously promoted an army of gifted managers who worked their way up from secretary.

The problem is, there aren't enough of these types to go around. So even legitimate superstars watch plenty of others get promoted simply due to, well, self-promotion. And right or wrong, these affronts make the rewards feel less legitimate.

What do you get when unqualified officers are promoted up the ladder? For one, bad managers—those who find themselves in charge of others not because of leadership talent, but because a broken system assumes that once they reach a certain personnel grade, they are somehow magically ready to supervise others. Not surprisingly, these managers don't know how to lead and care little about their subordinates.

The best and brightest don't make it to the top at the Agency for other reasons. For one, many simply don't hang around long enough. They jump ship after their first or second tour and move on to new careers.

That, and many of the good ones who do stay in the job actually love the job—the fundamentals of it, that is. These officers would rather be out on the street conducting operations—not sitting inside an office conducting staff meetings. So they resist managerial positions for as long as possible.

One more, perhaps flakier, reason why the good ones leave the Agency—they are so disappointed that such a foundation of US national security often seems weak and incompetent, they feel they can't rely on their own institutions to protect the country.

Ironically, the CIA doesn't seem to worry when officers leave, despite the enormous amounts of time and money invested in each one. The way they see it, a certain amount of churn just means a supply of fresh blood.

Such an attitude would make sense—especially in a

closed system—if the bad ones were resigning as well, thereby making room for new and improved officers. But as we shall see, this isn't the case, and the ones that *need improvement* typically stick around, like houseguests who can't take the hint. These folks know they're not welcome anymore, but they have no other place to go.

You simply can't get rid of them.

Lesson Twelve

Why the Bad Ones Stay

Agents rarely quit. Despite all the dangers and downsides, they know they have a pretty good gig.

C/Os are no different.

Most of the good ones leave early in their careers. The worst ones are fired or arrested. With sadly few exceptions, this leaves the leftovers—the mediocre, not-so-good-but-not-bad-enough-to-be-kicked-out-of-the-building extras.

As tragic as it is, the Agency has become a giant warehouse for dead wood—people who somehow slip into the system, never quit, never move on, and contribute virtually nothing to the mission. The saddest part of all is that most of these leftovers would've been dismissed years ago, had they worked virtually anywhere else.

The business of espionage is chock-full of unprofessionalism. Why? Because the services hire the wrong people, provide little supervision and oversight, and levy few consequences for bad behavior.

Then, the employees—normal, average humans that they are—exploit these weaknesses by doing the bare minimum necessary to remain in their positions as long as possible.

Still, why do so many stay? Perhaps more precisely,

why do they choose not to leave, despite all the crappy parts of the job?

For starters, many newbies arrive at the Agency with low expectations. Fresh hires are usually on their second careers, so they know all about bureaucracies and how they function, especially if they've come from another government job. Many already believe they won't make any impact, that nothing significant will ever change within the organization. To them, joining the CIA is not about fulfilling a life's calling but just about obtaining a secure federal job.

Other personnel become disappointed but choose to stay anyway—largely because of the generous benefits. So they settle in for the long haul. Their careers turn into marathons to reap those rewards, not sprints for glory or a means to make a mark on the world.

And let's face it. There sure are some plum rewards.

There's the money, of course. Don't believe any sob stories about Agency personnel as poor government servants—not when it comes to Case Officers, at least.

Sure, when compared to high tech or medicine, the starting salary may seem small, especially when most officers are on their second careers. But this is part of the CIA's grand plan of equality—everyone starts near the bottom. A few C/Os may boast about the pay cuts they took to come to the Agency. But most of them still receive generous salaries relative to their qualifications.

And the gifts keep on giving.

As in the military, more than just base salary determines how a total CIA compensation package measures up. C/Os receive ridiculously generous benefits when stationed overseas, where they spend the bulk of their careers. For some, collecting these benefits begins to dominate their lives.

All sorts of bumps and bonuses become available—from five to seventy-five percent more salary—depending on the danger, difficulty, and cost of living of your country. In developing countries, for example, C/Os are even compensated for the crime, dirty air, and lack of services.

And those hardship posts aren't as bad as you think. Because on top of the extra money, C/Os get other freebies, including a big house, a kitchen full of American appliances, twenty-four-hour security guards, satellite TV with American channels, and a high wall to keep out any local riff-raff. That, and the government pays for utilities and fixes anything at your residence that may break. Some houses even have swimming pools around back—jokingly referred to as "emergency water supplies."

When it comes to benefits, the government seems to have thought of everything.

In emergencies, they send employees on all-expenses-paid medevacs, dentevacs, and even "wackevacs," for psychological problems.

Come to think of it, it's amazing how many Frankfurt or London dentevacs coincided with an officer's child visiting those cities on spring break. Indeed, many C/Os dream up ways to regularly leave their hardship posts—one way or another—courtesy of good ol' Uncle Sugar, despite the fact that they receive free vacation tickets home each year, sometimes even *per diem*, for living in such treacherous places.

Even those who avoid hardship posts end up with plenty of extras. A nice, rich country still means additional pay to compensate for the high cost of living, which is usually tax-free. Housing will suffer relative to developing countries, of course—C/Os are likely to come home to a more-modest apartment, and paid vacations out of the country are out of the question, as they're living in a place where Third World C/Os take their own R&Rs.

As a sidebar, overseas housing can be an unpredictable part of Agency life. At first, you're relaxing in your backyard pool, reveling in the life of a colonial expat on the subcontinent. A blink later, and you're reassigned to Afghanistan, where the whole world hits rock-bottom—housing-wise, at least. Now, you're living in a ten-by-ten-foot room, ensconced in a seemingly concrete submarine, with no family and little freedom or privacy, surrounded by dozens of your closest colleagues. That, coupled with cobras and scorpions, malaria, mortars, rockets and suicide bombers, extreme heat and cold, earthquakes, violent monsoon storms, and seven-day work weeks makes for a fairly uncomfortable welcome party. It's the real deal, though. In southwestern Afghanistan, my team lived in a small, steel shipping container crammed with four bunk beds.

But back to all those goodies.

There's free tuition for kids at fancy international schools that can run thirty or forty grand a year. The tuition bill alone for a colleague with five kids came out to twice his annual salary. Without an acceptable option in country, C/Os are welcome to send them—free of charge—to a boarding school in Switzerland or the UK.

The perks extend to plenty more important things—like food. The government provides well-stocked commissaries that resemble a local Safeway in the middle of far-off, foreign countries. There, C/Os can find most of the American foods they thought they'd have to do without—fully subsidized, of course, so they won't have to experience any nasty sticker shock. Strangely, such commissaries exist even in developed, First-World regions, like Western Europe, where there are plenty of local supermarkets.

To further prevent any kind of cultural assimilation, commissaries often exist in US government-constructed, Little America communities, chock-full of suburban-style housing complexes, shops, and restaurants.

Indeed, the Agency recognizes that many employees didn't sign up to experience other cultures, and most wouldn't tolerate much actual hardship anyway, at least long-term. In this sense, hardship means buying unfamiliar products or living in local housing. Not too shabby.

Removed from the scary foreigners and their yucky food, these official communities live up to the common phrase we often uttered: "living in the bubble." Some happily stayed put therein for their whole tour.

Official vans shuttle employees from the housing compound to and from work, so no need to drive a car or step off the curb to catch a rusty taxi. Properly organized weekend excursions exist as well: trips to malls and restaurants for those too timid to venture out on their own.

And don't worry about going without prized possessions. The government pays to ship every last one, ten or twenty thousand pounds of stuff—cars, furniture, paintings—the whole shebang, no matter where you happen to end up. If you don't feel like sending your possessions overseas, they'll store them for you back in the US. As for me, like the good bohemian I was, I usually moved with two suitcases and a dog—much to the shock of my colleagues.

But perhaps the biggest pot of gold waits at the end of the rainbow—that is, the coveted pension and health care for life. As in the military, CIA officers are eligible to retire after twenty years of service, at which point they may collect an immediate annuity—which could be worth millions, depending on how long one lives. The army itself refers to the waiting—or rather, working—period as "doing time," which, in many cases, it is.

Like in an actual prison, most inmates are on their best behavior, trying to keep a clean record until their release date. This means they take few chances, think inside the box, and avoid doing anything that will rock the boat—in other words, they accomplish relatively little.

Over the course of a twenty-year career, a C/O, without much effort, should have stashed away a small fortune—if he managed his money wisely, that is, which, of course, many do not. But that's not entirely his fault. For example, the sky-high divorce rate can lead to hefty alimony and child-support payments. For these and other reasons, after years and years overseas in multiple, far-flung assignments, many C/Os are actually flat broke when they finally retire.

At least they had the job security to make it that far.

An Agency position is a guaranteed job for life. As one of the shrinks who interviewed me during the application process admitted: "The Agency is very much like that fancy school you went to—very hard to get into and very hard to be kicked out of."

How so?

First of all, very few employees are ever laid off.

Apparently, a few C/Os and analysts were downsized at the end of the Cold War, but that was a rare event.

Similarly, outside of committing a felony, very little (if anything) can get a C/O fired when it comes to office work. I never once heard of anyone being let go because of lackluster production.

In short, there are few consequences for bad behavior, poor performance, or even a bad economy, so there's no real need to excel. Instead, most officers flip on the cruise control and coast their way to the ends of their careers.

A few years ago, a *very* senior Agency official actually complained to a small group about the lack of churn among the rank and file—that too many officers were simply staying put—something he considered unhealthy for the organization. Interestingly enough, this happened a few short weeks before he himself was forced to resign for his own, now-public, bad behavior.

The CIA is full of extremely bad behavior—from outright felonies like committing espionage and stealing official funds, to falsifying cables and seducing subordinates. Some incidents go unpunished.

Why?

The clichéd good-old-boy network may be protecting the culprits, or perhaps the Agency just wants to avoid public scandals and lawsuits. I've even heard speculation that leadership fears punished officers could become disgruntled, switch sides, and volunteer to work for an opposition service. If true, this strange logic dictates that the Agency keep useless, even crooked, employees on the payroll simply for fear of the collateral damage of letting them go.

No matter the reason, it's a serious issue. In my time, we joked that you'd practically have to kill someone in the HQS cafeteria to ever get fired. Getting others killed, however—agents, even fellow C/Os—may not get you axed. There are officers still walking Agency hallways who have done just that.

Others have successfully gotten agents arrested, destroyed official property, been kicked out of countries, recruited fake agents, caused sources to quit because of bad tradecraft, lost thousands of dollars in agent salaries in taxis, and accidentally included Top Secret information about unilateral targeting priorities in official memos passed to host governments.

Their punishments? For most, a proverbial slap on the wrist. The Agency has a terrible short-term memory and is either quick to forgive and forget—or just doesn't care that much anymore.

Case in point: there once was a senior married C/O who was notorious for bedding female subordinates. Those in the know said his personnel file was inches thick, crammed with complaints from fellow officers, none of which seemed to affect his career in the least. Apparently, he was just too senior to touch.

For its part, the Agency required him to attend an intensive counseling-slash-therapy program. At the end of the program, he appeared to reach a breakthrough, convincing those around him that he'd been cured. The guy went so far as to hug the psychologist who'd been treating him—then grabbed her butt mid-embrace.

Crickets from the Agency.

Perhaps in part due to its willingness to turn a blind eye, infidelity is rather common at the Agency. It does get awful lonely on those long-term TDYs separated from your spouse. Hell, I know married officers who have fathered kids with foreign girlfriends, with virtually zero career consequences. Thankfully, some are at least decent enough to send periodic child support.

As mentioned, such bad behavior goes right up the chain to the highest levels of command. For every scandal among senior officials that actually makes the news, you can imagine how many similar events are systematically hushed up.

Unlike senior staff, journeymen C/Os are fairly expendable. Their slap on the wrist may also include a side dish of the Agency's official version of shunning. Depending on the offense—even for something as menial as producing bad polygraph results—the Agency may practice a form of internal exile of its employees.

Like Milton in the movie *Office Space*, these employees are shamefully banished to insignificant departments in far-off buildings, where they're left to rot, all in the hopes that they'll quit of their own volition, rather than on the Agency's dime.

When I walked through HQS, I truly believed the place would run better without most of its employees. But as in any good bureaucracy, each layer, once added, can never be eliminated.

The CIA rarely makes large-scale personnel changes. Instead, managers slap on a new metaphorical coat of paint to cover up the deeper problems and keep the place running for one more year—or, at least, until they retire. When and if they do attempt more systemic change, it's only out of absolute necessity and in a reactive manner. Meanwhile, the underlying foundation continues to crumble.

Here's the central paradox: One might think the enormous pay and benefits lavished on C/Os would lead to a much better result: happy and productive officers. But it seems to have the opposite effect.

Like any spoiled child, the more C/Os get—often simply for showing up—the more they want, the more they expect, and the less they work, the less they appreciate, and the less happy they become.

One of my biggest impressions from serving overseas was how unhappy most officers were. In my mind, we had the greatest job in the world. We had made it to the top—we were getting paid to travel the world and serve our country.

Yet most officers were not only obsessed with collecting every last penny of their salary and benefits, but they saw others simply as competition, gossiping about and back-stabbing their colleagues every chance they got. They compared any benefits they received and became furious when another seemed to receive more.

As previously noted, this may be intentional. C/Os are, ironically, hired in part because of their vulnerabilities. Ideally, satisfying these shortcomings will forge some kind of loyalty between the personnel and the organization, as officers will identify the Agency as their benefactor and become less likely to betray it or leave. The problem is, they *all* will be less likely to leave. And in a perfect world, some of them—especially the less-than-stellar ones—should pack up and go. As that senior official admitted: Churn is good.

In a perfect world, job security also seems like a good idea. Furnishing an environment in which employees don't have to worry about losing their jobs allows them to focus on the quality of their work.

Right?

A few may thrive in this scenario, of course. But the

majority of C/Os abuse the privilege by doing the bare minimum and skirting regulations.

To me, the CIA unintentionally proves that social assistance programs, such as long-term unemployment insurance, do not work—at least for those who are otherwise able-bodied. Its system shows that when a person has a guaranteed income, she will generally do as little as possible to guarantee her survival. Even the best and brightest don't have much of an internal engine to keep them motivated or even disciplined—especially when the system consists of all carrots and almost no sticks.

So maybe it's time to address the benefits packages at the Agency—that, as in politics, there's simply too much money sloshing around the system. Salaries are too high. Houses too big. Pensions too generous. At the very least, they're out of whack with what the employees are actually accomplishing on a daily basis when it comes to the job of national security.

But what about the importance of such benefits packages when attracting the best applicants?

It's a fair question. But still, come on. This is national security we're talking about. Something's definitely wrong if money is the primary driver of applicants—at least at an entity with such an uncommon mission. Better to attract fewer applicants for the right reasons than more applicants for the wrong reasons. Such a remarkable place can do better.

And such a remarkable career, even without all the freebies, would continue to receive truckloads of applications.

But maybe these are naïve goals. Maybe this is merely a wake-up call from the real world: there are no actual careers with higher callings and no real people who fill them. Maybe this really is all there is.

Crap.

I sure hope not.

Lesson Thirteen

The CIA at War

The whole country rallied behind the Agency after 9/11. Ordinary citizens sent letters expressing encouragement, even offering to use their unique talents to help its mission. My personal favorite? A dentist declared his expertise in inflicting pain and volunteered to help out in any way necessary.

All this goodwill lasted a few years until the war in Iraq and the WMD debacle. Much has been written about those events, some of which points to the use of intelligence for political objectives.

While both Iraq and Afghanistan were initially overwhelming military victories, the US government was unprepared for the sudden transition from warfare to occupation and reconstruction. While soldiers often talk about the fog of war, this was a *fog of peace.*

In Iraq, after the end of major combat operations in 2003, Baghdad station staff ran around like a chicken with its head cut off. No one knew who was in charge or what to do next. As expected, this resulted in loads of meetings, plenty of talking, and little actually getting accomplished. The few instructions sent down from above were revised every day, due to the rapidly changing events on the ground.

Part of this chaos resulted from the shock of the

whole conflict ending so quickly—the rest from lack of preparation for what to do next.

Despite what Americans did or didn't accomplish, Iraqis complained that little had changed. They shook their heads at the bombed-out buildings around Baghdad—daily reminders of America's weakness, they said, and why so few had faith in the new boss. Saddam, they added, would have leveled those structures immediately, if only to show that he was all-powerful and could rebuild everything.

The US government also didn't help itself in the way it treated the locals in the war zones.

On an army base in eastern Afghanistan, soldiers test-fired howitzers on the slopes of nearby mountains, dislodging rocks and dirt and raining debris on villages below.

A few hours after one such practice session, an assault rifle was fired onto our base from the vicinity of a nearby village, hitting a civilian. The incident was chalked up to a small-time terrorist attack. It seemed to me, at least, that the shooter was likely an ordinary Afghan, driven to take this action because of soldiers wreaking havoc on his home.

And then, there was the lack of preparation. With the unexpectedly quick end to the Iraq war, scarce resources were allocated to Baghdad station for the reconstruction phase.

In fact, my branch didn't even have a car for me to meet our Iraqi counterparts, so I borrowed one from the Iraqis. That meant that each day, I drove myself half-way across post-war Baghdad to Iraqi HQS in a beat-up, thin-skinned, bald-tired SUV, an M-4 resting on my lap and just hoping that truck wouldn't break down.

And that's not the worst of it. Once I arrived, all I could provide my counterparts was a handful of lame excuses—yes, we have money coming soon—yes, we're working on a real plan for the future—not surprisingly, the locals never believed me.

Resources that were provided seemed out of whack. A few months after major hostilities ended, Baghdad station received a brand new set of fancy office furniture, the pieces awkwardly arriving a few days after the mortars and rockets started falling, signaling a brand new phase of the conflict.

In our defense, the enemy was also unprepared for the end of the war. It took them several months to comprehend all that had happened, regroup, and eventually shift from major hostilities with a superpower to a localized guerilla war/terrorist insurgency, depending on how the story was spun.

But until that time, it did, indeed, seem like the war had ended, at least on the surface. The infamous al-Rashid hotel hosted discos, where hundreds of young Western soldiers and officials hit the dance floor. As in Afghanistan, we drove ourselves around Baghdad, shopped, and ate in local restaurants.

Meanwhile, station provided Washington reams of reports stating that the enemy had not been defeated but was simply preparing for the next phase of war. In fact, the senior official who famously delivered this bad news was recalled for his Debbie Downer attitude. Instead, policymakers back home were so busy celebrating that major hostilities had ended, they never even gazed out at the horizon. Alarms were going off all over the place, but no one was listening.

Then, while I brushed my teeth, the first mortar hit,

several hundred feet away. I dove under the bed and wondered if this was all she wrote.

During a lull in the shooting, I ran to our nearby office where some were still working. For these seasoned guys, mortars had no effect. The dudes hadn't even moved from their desks. My immediate boss, a retired Army Ranger, sat before a wall-sized glass window and barely glanced up from his computer. "Looks like rain tonight," he mumbled.

It was then that car bombs started exploding. The number of armed attacks soared. Mortar and rocket strikes became a regular event. Hesco barriers and thick concrete slabs went up around important locations.

We sat outside our hooches after dark and listened as the Air Force flew over the city, machine-gunning any threats on the streets. Nearby, a European security team shot at stray dogs that wandered through the neighborhood.

The peacetime pause had ended. While we'd temporarily beaten them into submission, the US military hadn't destroyed the enemy. Many Iraqi resisters had survived, melted away, and regrouped to fight another day. To them, the real war was only just beginning.

And thanks to the power vacuum we'd created, other regional powers jumped in, too.

While I didn't support the decision to go to war in the first place, I figured if we were in it, we'd better win. But in our current condition, that mentality was doomed from the start. The US could easily defeat a Third World army. But to think we could ever remake—or even rebuild—a place like Iraq? Plain foolishness.

It's one thing to attack a country, destroy its infrastructure, overthrow a regime. It's quite another to replace that regime with a Western-style democracy—or a Western-style *anything*, especially in the East. It's simply illogical to assume that any nation is ready for a system that is foreign to them.

After all, the last authoritarian regime hadn't flown in from outer space. It sprang up organically inside the country—from the people themselves. Saddam's regime survived for decades because governments reflect their populations—their history, their culture, their personality—in the end, governments reflect the ways in which their societies function.

Like humans, every nation's maturity level, if you will, reflects its stage of social and economic development. Some are younger. Others are older. Younger nations require strong parents to teach them, keep them in line, even tell them what to do. So it's no coincidence that these places tend to foster authoritarian regimes. Sure, it's unfair, but most of the locals aren't prepared to handle the hard decisions required to run a country. We see this all the time, as nations attempt a democratic experiment, only to return immediately to their old ways of governing.

The same is true in Afghanistan. As unpopular as the opinion is, in my experience, the country almost needs a regime like the Taliban to run things. Because even if we hunted down every single fighter, the group would somehow reanimate. Why? Because we're not even touching the mentality that spawned and sustained the group as we take out its representatives. Locals look to the Taliban because, in such a wild and unruly place, they're strong, decisive, and they can get things done—much like a firm parent attempting to straighten out a reckless kid.

In Afghanistan, a free and open democratic system where citizens decide in matters of government is reversely anachronistic—or grossly premature. Historically speaking, countries naturally implement democratic structures *only after* developing an educated middle class, the rule of law, and a strong commitment to private property.

Iraq and Afghanistan have none of these. Not yet, anyway.

So all the money and bullets in the world will not move these countries forward in time—unless we completely break them, WWII-style. That means carpet-bombing cities, perhaps dropping nuclear weapons, in order to rebuild from scratch. And we're not willing to use such extreme measures, not now, at least. So the US will forever be foiled in its attempt to remake other countries simply because they're in different stages of evolution and therefore don't share our values.

Some may find this ostensibly isolationist opinion ironic, especially considering my own overseas career. But it's one thing for the US to be actively engaged in the world with diplomats, aid workers, even intelligence collectors, in order to protect and promote our national interests—and quite another for our government to embark on uninformed and costly foreign conquests that often end badly.

The decision to go to war was a conscious one, made by politicians and bureaucrats who supposedly know best, particularly in terms of foreign policy.

And maybe that's the core of the problem. Conducting sound foreign policy isn't just about identifying threats and prioritizing national interests. High-ranking officials must also choose the right options for dealing with those threats, based on a supposed deep knowledge and understanding of our enemies.

But that's not how it works.

In so many of these cases, the decision-makers didn't utilize their own massive intelligence resources to even try to understand what was actually going on. Instead, they famously formed opinions and policies *before*—and even instead of—ever reading the analysis. Indeed, some have asked, why even bother with an intelligence service if no one's going to use it?

But perhaps their biggest shortcoming is simple naïveté. Many of our *enlightened* leaders know all about history, politics, the military and its capabilities. They've participated in day-long junkets to personally meet with foreign counterparts. But they fundamentally do not understand the countries they are invading.

Many come from cushy jobs in academia and think tanks and reside in affluent neighborhoods like Georgetown and McLean, Virginia—far removed from the countries we're invading. Most have never lived overseas, never watched how ordinary people think and act, never sunk themselves deep into other worlds far different from their own.

Such components are vitally important to success in any foreign policy.

Instead, decision-makers subscribe to the Western notion that everyone, even those entrenched in far-off, foreign lands, thinks as they do. In this mindset, they can't comprehend the enormous differences between the US and the rest of the world, or how these differences affect behavior and cultural mindset. Instead, our country continues to learn these lessons the hard way through war after ridiculous war.

While I served in South Asia, our station hosted a senior NSC official. Although a political appointee, he was supposedly an expert on the region, even more so than those on the ground. And yet after a casual conversation wherein I mentioned the relatively common practice of local madrassas brainwashing young people to become religious fanatics rather than educating them, I overheard him excitedly relating our conversation to a colleague back home, as if he had just received groundbreaking intelligence.

To add insult to injury, Congress is often the weakest link in the chain of government. Surprise, surprise. These days, many members are elected not for their technocratic skills, but as the result of voter emotion regarding their positions on single issues. Uninformed and inexperienced, these officials are typically the most unqualified professionals at any level of government.

We got to see this up close during congressional visits to overseas installations and military bases. Everyone dreaded these obligatory visits as complete wastes of time—except, of course, the actual visitors. These yahoos flew to the other side of the world, usually in first-class or via special military aircraft, spent a whirlwind day or two visit, then proudly reported back to their constituents that they'd not only visited the troops, but they'd seen the ground truth for themselves.

Nothing was further from the truth.

Stations shut down for days whenever these visitors showed up. Puffed up on special treatment back home, congressional visitors invariably demanded personal briefings from the COS, meetings with the C/Os and local counterparts, and the compulsory "windshield tour" of the town. Maybe throw in a little shopping for trinkets, *et voilà*! They're overseas experts—never mind the fact that they'd been chaperoned by station personnel every step of the way.

As C/Os, there was no way to avoid these boondoggles, no matter how much actual work we had to do. Elected officials often control the purse strings, so you better believe it was all hands on deck every visit.

Worse yet, Congress wasn't the only group insisting on a visit. After 9/11, planeloads of US government officials arrived in war zones to see some action, forming a non-stop conveyer belt of visits. On their end, the trips became rites of passage, tests of manhood, extra bullet-points on their performance reviews. For us, they were simply foolish wastes of time.

On the surface, the CIA welcomes these visits—especially by those with real authority over budget and operations. So stations perform cheerfully benign dog and pony shows while smiling broadly and treating each guest like royalty. But we celebrated when the wheels finally went up, and we could all go back to work.

The war in Afghanistan was similar to Iraq: a shockingly quick military victory, followed by a brief period of deceptive peace and false hope, finished off by a never-ending, bloody stalemate.

During the interim period of quiet, we moved freely, met with locals, did our jobs.

Meanwhile, the enemy didn't waste the break in the action. The fighters regrouped, learned our deepest fears, and concocted an effective insurgency, largely based on those fears.

It was all over once they started kidnapping people and cutting off their heads on camera.

The enemy knew we had no stomach for a dirty

war. The US government wanted clean victory, clean death—no mess, no fuss. After Vietnam, US policymakers knew the effects that horrific images would have on the country—that the American people wouldn't tolerate significant casualties from another messy, drawn-out war.

So when the enemy finally regrouped, we were locked down. It was Iraq all over again.

In Afghanistan, we hunkered down on fortified compounds, going out only when absolutely necessary and even then with a contingent of heavily-armed security. These former military personnel were great in a firefight, but they had only basic-level understanding of the environment, tradecraft, and operational matters. They stood out when they should have tried to blend in, flexing their muscles instead of using their minds to avoid trouble in the first place. Locals saw them coming from a mile away as they sped down streets in armored SUVs. Their aggressive techniques caused more trouble than they avoided—so much for clandestine operations or flying under the radar. Soldiers and intel officers are completely different animals with completely different MOs. Forcing the two professions to mix often doesn't work out well, and Afghanistan proved no exception.

While some security officers were good guys, my experience with them further disproved a military superhero myth, including the notion that an ability to do fifty push-ups signifies any sort of wisdom about the world.

Eventually, the stalemate became institutionalized. Both sides settled in for the long haul, knowing the balance of power would likely never change.

CIA officers, especially those working counterterrorism issues, like to say that trouble spots provide them job security. They'll add, tongue firmly planted in cheek, that they hope the bad guys will continue to survive in some form or other—at least until their kids graduate from college.

In a sense, these hopes have come true—the US has been involved in seemingly endless wars for decades.

Why?

Idealistic reasons include ensuring peace and prosperity in some of the most dangerous and neglected places on earth and combatting poverty and extremism with hard and soft power. The cynical take? To build schools so foreign nationals won't blow up airplanes.

At the same time, some folks are getting rich from these wars. Retired government and military officials operate beltway bandits and private security companies which are deeply involved in running the wars. And they have no interest in the wars ever ending.

Ironically, this situation mirrors what's happening on the other side—the Taliban, al-Qa'ida, ISIL, *et al*, also run their businesses in this manner. In essence, these organizations operate like giant companies, though with far-more nefarious products—selling drugs, kidnapping for ransom, and fundraising from wealthy regional donors. Their leaders get plenty rich from the wars, too.

So while it began as a noble cause, The War on Terror has devolved into a self-sustaining, commercial enterprise, contracted out by both sides to third-party, for-profit proxies who supply, report, and fight for money.

War has morphed into a business. And business is booming.

From the highest officials and ideologues, to the lowliest security guards and suicide bombers, the wars are now largely about making money. Some are in it for the millions, others for a few bucks a month. But the longer any conflict lasts, the more money that is spent—and the better the business.

On our side, money flows from Washington and a freshly-updated conspiracy, "the Military-*Intelligence* Complex."

On the other side, it comes from wealthy donors in Saudi Arabia and the Gulf, Pakistan, and other Muslim countries who see extremists as the armed wing of their religion. Money trickles down to jihadi commanders, soldiers, and facilitators, who make the fighting possible. These are hired guns, contractors who signed up largely for the paycheck. Most have no idea what they're even fighting for. But where else can they make a few hundred dollars a month in an otherwise-destitute land? Some parents are so desperate, they'll even sell their kids to extremist groups as suicide bombers.

The growth of even-more ruthless groups, such as ISIL, is largely a matter of money as well. These groups pay their fighters more. It's that simple. Ditching one group for another is basically a corporate move.

And therein lies the rub—nobody gets paid if they don't conduct attacks—no matter how trivial or insignificant. Indeed, if you only read the news, you'd think these war-zone countries were practically on fire, sizzling with dozens of attacks every day. But like report-writing, it's all about the numbers, quantity over quality, and so many of the attacks are small-scale and insignificant. Regardless of who actually attacked what, several different groups will try to claim credit for every attack. It's in their financial best interests to do so.

The importance of finance reflects the increasing disinterest of those involved. In other words, the more you have to pay someone to do their job, even if that job means going to war, the less likely their hearts are really in it. Yet the reliance on big money has become routinized, a regular part of the cost of doing business. Because everyone expects it, few will go without a significant financial incentive.

The Agency is no exception.

While most would agree that our cause is just, money, rather than ideology, currently dominates the CIA's role in modern warfare. The Agency has become the recipient, middleman, and distributor of ungodly sums.

The salary and benefits required to motivate an average officer to deploy to a war zone are enormous. But they draw some of the personnel over and over again, so much so, that the majority of the assignments are performed by a minority of officers.

The wars could have functioned as external inputs with the potential to change the CIA's dysfunctional closed system. Instead, the government decided from the very start that they didn't want the country—or even its employees—to feel significant side effects from the wars. It wanted an oxymoronically *pain-free* conflict, which reflects how the Agency treats its war zone personnel.

The CIA lavishes money and benefits on anyone, staff or contractor, willing to spend a few months or years living in a concrete bunker on the other side of the world, enduring loneliness, isolation, and occasional mortars. Even low-level officers can bank a hundred thousand dollars from a one-year assignment.

Danger and Differential bonus pay almost doubles a staffer's base salary. Then, there's overtime.

In war zones, stations and bases expect personnel to work seven days a week, twelve hours a day. Well, "work" is probably not accurate. They expect them *to be at their desks* for that period of time. Whether they do any actual work is ultimately up to them. Most C/Os return to the office after dinner and on weekends simply because of peer pressure. There's a war on, for Christ's sake! How does it look when you put your feet up? Even with nothing to do, officers are expected to be in the office. And that means collecting overtime.

A quick glance around the room revealed plenty of officers furiously banging away on their computers. But upon closer examination, I found that most of them were merely gossiping with friends and colleagues around the world on the Agency's internal chat system. This feature, originally intended to streamline the communications process, has turned into yet another distraction, used far more for social than operational purposes.

There are plenty of other war zone perks, including all-expenses-paid housing and food. From three, often luxurious meals per day—steak and lobster anyone?—coupled with all-you-can-eat and drink snacks and energy drinks, topped off with business-class chartered flights to and from the locations, this is not your father's war zone. A support officer at a small base in Afghanistan confided that the cost of providing Red Bull and Gatorade alone ran five thousand dollars a month.

The CIA also takes precautions you would never dream of. In western Afghanistan, they actually sent out a hygiene team to measure the amount of bacteria that might be collecting in the faucet sinks, though everyone used bottled water, even to brush their teeth.

Not gonna lie, the perks are pretty sweet. But all these benefits merely assuage the more weak-kneed officers' fears about agreeing to the tour.

Others are downright shameless about the perks. On the ride to town from the airport, a newly arrived senior officer in Kabul flat-out admitted he had no interest in actually getting involved in any high-risk operations. He was only in country for one year, he said, and only for the money.

He was not alone. Some officers used war zone bonuses to make up for years of wasteful spending, others to leap-frog economic classes. They serve to pay off mortgages or acquire luxury items. One C/O planned to purchase a two-hundred-thousand-dollar sports car when he finished his war-zone tour. Another stayed in Kabul for several years to pay off his son's entire college education. After a few drinks, some even admitted they just wanted to get away from their "pain-in-the-ass" spouses.

In Baghdad, I ran into a former instructor who had accepted a relatively low-level job in station. He explained his decision simply: "I need the money. I've got two kids in college and my wife just had a five-thousand-dollar facelift." Even after working for twenty years, he had almost nothing saved.

War zone assignments have turned into box-checking exercises where little real work is done. Many just collect the perks, get their tickets punched, and leverage the experience into choice follow-on assignments.

Still, opportunistic officers aren't half as bad as the so-called war correspondents, posing for the cameras in their ill-fitting flak jackets to film a segment from atop the nicest hotel they can find, then fleeing back to Paris or Dubai. Three days in the war zone, and boom—national heroes and mission accomplished. The whole world was fooled. In truth, they likely never left that comfy hotel but merely dispatched stringers to interview locals and capture footage—another great war correspondent reporting from the front lines.

I knew it had reached this stage of complacency when I overheard an Agency analyst speaking with the station gunsmith in Kabul. She complained that the sights on her M-4 rifle needed adjustment—this from an officer with no need for an M-4, as she would never leave the compound, let alone fire the weapon. Still, it fit snugly into her make-believe war-zone experience—where she could pretend, at least in the office, to be GI Jane for a few weeks. The Agency issued firearms to everyone so they could feel like they were a part of the fight, not to mention the high-speed pics all kitted out to impress the folks back home.

The hypocrisy of it all drove me to write the following note to a HQS colleague while in eastern Afghanistan:

> *The guy sitting next to me is a spaz. Like everyone else, he is hopped up on Coke, coffee, chewing tobacco, and Red Bull all day long. I said to the support officer, "Can we please take away the Red Bull? Everyone here is so hyperactive." Another officer piped up: "Of course, we're hyperactive. We live in a war zone!" I just laughed. Most of these guys have never even left the compound—they might as well still be at HQS. They have virtually nothing to do with this place, this country, or this war. They run around all day long in a concrete bunker with little work to do—or at least any work that makes an actual difference in this Neolithic desert.*

> *They feel tremendous peer pressure to stay chained to the office all day and night. Some even eat meals at their desks, like the fate of the world rests on them being in front of the computer. They're desperate for a good performance review so they can leverage this ridiculous assignment into something pleasant and fun—to try to prove that the entire year wasn't the biggest waste of their lives. All this joy takes place in a politically correct kindergarten. I am in the office but not of the office. Anything that I say is taken literally. There's no understanding of subtlety or sarcasm. If I joke about someone, others try desperately to defend him. If I say something negative about the place, I'm an uninspired, unmotivated traitor who isn't here for the cause. We've worked ourselves into such a frenzy. It's like a religious crusade. But everyone's just in a massive state of denial. Mostly because it's all a massive waste of time, money, and people. This place has turned me into a nihilist.*

For me, the hardest part was getting on the plane to the war zones. I knew the entire world would change the next day, and I'd have to adjust once again to a totally different reality. Though I'd spent years in war zones, I wondered what fresh hell waited for me on the other side. Maybe my luck would finally run out.

Lining up to board the chartered flights, we looked like a group of escaped prisoners who'd just been recaptured. Most were quiet and stared at their shoes. They seemed annoyed or afraid—as if trying to remember why they'd ever agreed to this in the first place.

One time while waiting for a flight to Kabul, we watched as an attractive young woman and her designer dog exited a private jet. She passed by us—a long line of mostly fit, bearded men in cargo pants and boonie hats—and smiled uncomfortably. As she disappeared around a corner, I murmured to myself, "I'm on the wrong side of this picture."

But there was no going back.

Twenty-four hours later, we arrived in Kabul, having never left the plane. Considering the distance, it's probably the easiest flight we'd ever take—we never saw a single passport or customs official until our return to the US. That being said, we flew half-way around the world to a poor, small, relatively unimportant country that had—bafflingly—taken so many of our people and resources. Even after landing, the same thought plagued me: "What am I doing here?"

But despite all those benefits, the CIA still couldn't get enough volunteers for war zone assignments. And because they couldn't sweeten the pot with more juicy carrots, they tried some pointy sticks.

A few years ago, the Seventh Floor instituted a policy that mid-level officers couldn't be promoted to senior ranks without completing a war zone assignment.

Such an edict was apparently considered too draconian, however, so in time, the requirement was watered-down. These days, you don't have to be *physically located* in an actual war zone to get credit for a war zone assignment. That there's logic—US government-style. You can serve your sentence as a form of home-confinement by taking a Washington, DC-based desk position, as long as it technically supports a war zone.

Even still, there are plenty of officers who won't serve anywhere outside of Europe. Their punishment? Not much. Maybe they're put in the penalty box for a year or two, forced to sit on a desk at HQS. Then—back to Rome!

The *refuseniks* have their reasons for refusing hardship tours, of course. And unlike the military, the Agency won't fire or prosecute them simply because they won't take a certain assignment.

Before this policy was handed down, around twenty-five percent of officers were serving the vast majority of the war zone assignments. Indeed, a regular band of hard-core volunteers, mostly contractors, have, for whatever reason—money, comradery, less need for tradecraft, distance from the flagpole, a desire to get away from a spouse—made war zones their regular gig.

Again, not surprising. Where else can these folks make a thousand dollars a day with relatively little education? Like their counterparts on the other side of the war—certainly not back home.

Meanwhile, Washington continues to throw more money at the problems, hoping they will somehow resolve themselves.

After 9/11 and the Iraq War, the CIA was unable to staff the new bases that had popped up in the Middle East and South Asia.

So the Agency happily accepted gobs of congressional money to hire heaps of new Case Officers. Training classes swelled in size by five or six times. The new groups were enormous, unruly, and often unqualified. Failure rates went through the roof. Still, true to Agency form, those that didn't graduate weren't fired—they were simply offered other jobs within the organization.

Ironically, larger class sizes actually depleted the number of viable candidates. But because the CIA still needed to fill their billets, they were forced to lower the bar.

In the nineteen-nineties, for example, C/O applicants were required to have a minimum 3.5 GPA. This standard was eventually lowered to today's mandate of 3.0. Such a marker is not written in stone, however. Some sneak in with far less.

One colleague with a shockingly low 2.5 GPA transitioned through internal channels from a position as finance officer. Today, he is a full-fledged Case Officer, serving alongside his more-legitimate brethren. It probably didn't hurt that his mom also worked in the personnel office.

The thing is, the Agency was willing to fudge the standards for both personnel and budgetary reasons. In the aftermath of 9/11, they needed to get as many on board as quickly as possible, not only to man stations, but because they'd face budget cuts without high numbers. If they were unable to meet their quotas, Congress would cut funding, since such a failure would translate that they didn't need so many new people—whether they could find the people they *actually* needed was not Congress's problem. Hence, lowered standards won the day.

Due to the ongoing wars, the Recruitment Center now hires more applicants with military experience, which contributes to the melding of the CIA and the military. In theory, these candidates are tough, adaptable, and gung-ho, willing to take orders and go to dangerous locations.

In reality, they are just as high maintenance as other applicants. After all, they're not only military vets, but they're government organization vets. They know how to work the system for personal survival—how to play the game, how to stress appearance over accomplishment, and how bare minimum effort can lead to advancement—all while counting the days to retirement.

The military emphasis on rank, protocol, and formality has changed the culture of the Agency from relatively laid-back to more corporate, humorless, and by-the-book—needless to say, less fun. There is less nuance and sophistication among the workforce and more of a tendency to see the world in terms of black or white. These dramatic changes have made operations less effective, as the business of espionage doesn't follow clear-cut methodology, existing instead in the proverbial grey area. To be a successful officer requires freedom, creativity, and out-of-the-box thinking, not following orders in a rigid hierarchy.

As previously noted, a Case Officer is also a solo job. Most decisions on the street are made when no one else is around—no commander watching out or telling you what to do, no battle-buddy or teammate to back you up. Indeed, human intelligence is, in many ways, incompatible with military structure.

As a result, there's a clear difference between pre-and post-9/11 hires. Class One included only a handful of military vets. In recent years, far more new officers have military experience.

The truth is, the DO is most effective in times of peace. While the OSS was forged by war, the CIA was formed during peacetime. It does best in cold—not hot—wars, where the rules are clear, the environment relatively stable, and the bad guys easily identified. It flourishes when C/Os can go about their business without the distractions of bombs and mortars. When they can actually apply their expertise, since active war zones require far less traditional tradecraft.

When it comes right down to it, the Agency loves the world of make-believe—where you can be whomever you want and act however you wish with few lasting consequences. Traditionally, C/Os have been a unique band of laid-back, free-thinking, pseudo intellectuals and *bon vivants* who believed they had the world figured out. They played spy games with chess-like moves in make-believe-type environments and cared little about any harmful side effects.

That's what peacetime offers: Fewer lives are at stake, and you likely won't be shot at much. This is also true of agents—only a tiny percentage of agents ever get caught in the first place, and peacetime only lessens that risk.

Structurally, the CIA shares characteristics with both the State Department and the military. Prior to 9/11, it leaned closer to State, but in recent years, the pendulum has swung in the opposite direction.

The wars brought with them an introduction to real-world consequences—that despicable word. C/Os' lives and decisions were suddenly more in play. Make-believe was over.

But believe it or not, despite my earlier cynicism, to me the biggest problem with the CIA at war isn't the perks or the personnel—it's the attitude of the war.

Wars may happen thousands of miles away, but how they are fought reflects the nature of home countries and the people within.

The 9/11 attacks generated tremendous patriotism, a

thirst for revenge, and the desire to fight a just war. This also attracted a highly motivated and dedicated brand of officer to the war zones—at least, in the beginning.

These emotions were soon wasted, however, when it became apparent that Bin Ladin would stay holed up a lot longer than we'd planned, and again when Iraq became more important than Afghanistan.

Suddenly, no one cared much about that just war.

If the US could basically turn off the war in Afghanistan, many government personnel concluded that it must not be that important. After all, it wasn't WWII. The far-off country was no longer an existential threat to the homeland. A relatively small number of personnel could handle the situation on the ground, and the folks back home were told to "go shopping."

The lack of interest took its toll on the intelligence community as well. In Afghanistan, the CIA's priorities changed from collecting the best possible intelligence, even making an impact, to simply avoiding casualties. Indeed, personnel quickly realized that it had become far more important to have a clean operational record, to hunker down and hold the fort, than to try to accomplish anything significant.

Unfortunately, this cynical attitude has since spread to CIA operations around the globe. The Agency was already prone to risk aversion—it's the nature of all massive bureaucracies. But the most recent wars have made it all but institutionalized. Now, at nearly every station in the world, the predominant attitude has become: There is far more to lose than gain by taking risks.

So the wars continue, but these days, they are largely conducted on auto pilot. The adrenaline wore off years ago. Most of the goodwill was wasted as stoicism—even indifference—has set in.

Today, both the country and the Agency care about only one thing: retaining the *status quo*.

At least we're safe. I guess.

Lesson Fourteen

The Agency Makes You a Nihilist

At the end of *The In-Laws*, Peter Falk, when explaining why he's quitting the CIA, declares, "I've had it. I'm tired. It's over. I tell you something else . . . I don't believe in this crap anymore."

For most of the movie, he radiated confidence and sarcasm. He was sincere about the job. But life in general seemed silly, so he didn't take it too seriously. That was the character I wanted to be in my own career—and I naively expected to meet a few like him in the organization.

But by the end of the movie, reality had caught up to Falk. He had seen too much. So many things had changed, and the job just wasn't that fun anymore. By the end of my career, I could empathize with those feelings.

For the record, I started my Agency career as one of those dewy-eyed, naïve idealists that spill out into the hallway during breaks in CIA 101. At that time, I could imagine no greater job, no higher calling, than the secret brotherhood. The Agency was going to be the center of my world. I knew, based on my background, education, and personality, that I was born to be a Case Officer—and I still feel that way years after leaving.

I believed then, and I still do now, that you should pick a team and stick with it—and the CIA was my team.

This belief relates to my idea of patriotism, which I realize to some is a controversial, even laughable, concept these days. But in my mind, patriotism doesn't mean blind loyalty, my country right or wrong. It simply means standing up for the group to which you belong—because it's supposed to represent your deepest-held beliefs—and honoring those who sacrificed to make things better for you.

University taught me to be an idealist, to expect that people and situations live up to some higher purpose. Obviously, a secluded and secure campus is an easy place to practice such a philosophy.

As I've pointed out, these ideas set me up for a quite a fall.

The CIA taught me to be a realist—some would say a cynic, or even a nihilist. Traces of disappointment appeared soon after walking in the building, gathered fuel during my first tour under that dreadful COS. Day by day, the work burned the naïve idealism out of me. Perhaps it came relatively late in life, but the Agency forced me to grow up and live in the real world—admittedly, a harsh, extreme version of the real world. But I'm a much happier person because of that education.

After years in the espionage business, one of the most important lessons I learned was to enter into a situation, not with expectations of how things should be, but with a willingness to recognize how they truly are.

High expectations will leave you forever disappointed. You will move from place to place, perpetually hoping the next one will be better, that it will live up to your unrealistic expectations. But it never will. Nothing will ever be good enough. There will always be some fault to pick at, some excuse to keep moving. Or you'll give up trying, coming up instead with plenty of plausible reasons to never leave your comfort zone.

In the ideal world, you live like a little kid, holding your breath until you get exactly what you want, taking your football and going home when it doesn't happen. Life becomes one big coping mechanism simply because reality is too disappointing.

While you may keep your so-called personal standards in the process, you'll miss out on heaps of adventure along the way. To me, that's the school of idealism in a nutshell—it's a delight at university but a nightmare in the real world.

It's also why so many CIA officers quit such an extraordinary job after only one or two tours, why others leave before training even begins. The whole experience is simply too deflating—a fanciful delusion crushed by sobering reality. Here they thought they had joined an almost supernatural organization, one that is feared and respected around the world—and they weren't even issued a shoe-phone, let alone a license to kill. When the often-humdrum reality rears its ugly head, it's just too much for these dreamers to accept. And it's not even the yawning mouth of boredom that gets to them, but the letdown—that wide, echoing chasm between expectation and reality.

I almost sank into that void myself.

My idealistic side hated the Agency. The expectations were too high, the reality too low. My impulse told me to get out, to run away, far and fast. How could I stay in such a disappointing place?

It would be hard to work for long at the CIA as an idealist or a dreamer. After you look behind the curtain, you will never be the same. For some, the wake-up call is simply too much.

In truth, I reminded myself, those officers who leave early *did* join the world's premier spy agency—at least, relative to what else is out there. But the fact that the organization still exists in the real world—their idealism wouldn't accept such a distinction. Could mine?

The school of realism demands you compare what you've been given in life to how life *really* is, what's present on the ground, rather than what's in your head. In this world, there's no such thing as an ideal job, an omniscient organization, or even a perfect situation.

In a Dickensian sort of way, the Agency is, simultaneously, one of the best and one of the worst places anywhere. Depending on the day, the officer, the station, the operation, and—perhaps most importantly—your expectations, either assessment could be correct. And you just have to accept this strange dichotomy.

So in the transition from idealism to realism, I learned that it was me—or at least my perspective—that had to change, not those around me. It was up to me to accept the world as it is, rather than continually holding it hostage to what I wanted it to be. Similarly, I learned to focus on all that I had already been given in life, rather than the few items still missing. These changes made for a healthier perspective.

Yes, it's scary sometimes to watch the sausage being made in the US government, to realize that few institutions can be trusted and that the world is often a meaningless place. But if that's the truth as it actually is, why not embrace it? After all, isn't that life's (and even the Agency's) main purpose—to find the truth?

Fortunately, I learned these lessons in time to grab

an oar and keep on paddling, rather than jump ship completely.

Because from the viewpoint of the school of realism, the CIA's still a very special place, and I can think of no other career that tops it. I've even talked a few despondent first-tour officers off the gangplank with this perspective.

That's the world I joined when I decided to swallow my expectations and stay at the Agency. I chose peaceful co-existence over a fight or flight response. For me, it made all the difference.

I moved my career to a smaller, less bureaucratic office that let me keep one foot inside the closed system and one in the real world. It was a good balance and a healthy compromise—perhaps a synthesis, if you're a fan of dialectics. I became much happier going to work every day, and I stayed at the Agency many more years.

At its roots, there's nothing fundamentally wrong with the CIA or how it was set up. Its founders, like those of the country, did a bang-up job. But humans rarely stay the course, and successors have spoiled a good thing for little real reason.

Most agree that the CIA must improve when it comes to hiring skilled officers, providing top-notch training, and collecting credible intelligence. This responsibility rests with its people, the lifeblood of the organization. But perhaps the Agency will only succeed in doing so with a better pool of candidates or even a different societal *zeitgeist*—when patriotism, sacrifice, and identity with country become common cultural features once again.

Eventually, I did leave—largely because everyone has a breaking point, and as I mentioned previously, working at the CIA can be a lot like a bad relationship. Despite the peace that realism brings, after a while, it becomes very difficult to stay true to who you are and to care like you should, especially when it comes to the people.

As Groucho Marx said, "I don't want to belong to any club that will accept people like me as a member." My take is: I don't want to stay—too long at least—in any place that claims such an important mission, especially when I bought into that mission wholeheartedly, since the other personnel will inevitably leave you in the lurch. It's bound to grind you down eventually.

In truth, the feeling was mutual. Agency managers could also tell I just didn't believe in this crap anymore.

At the same time, I remembered that it's still a big, beautiful world, and no single entity could possibly have everything I want in life. That other, even more profound, people and places outside the Agency are just waiting. This can take a while, though.

My perspective disintegrated overseas, where I was surrounded, day after day, by agents and officers with some of the basest character traits. Eventually, this led to a belief that such personas were the norm, that most human beings were just no good.

Every single day, I reported on the worst possible degenerates, horrible things they'd done, their plans to do even more of them. I was bombarded by war, terrorism, drugs and crime, and I began to believe that bad guys existed around every corner, that no part of any country was safe, that the world was a horrible, dystopian place that could explode at any moment.

So I left.

I left the Agency while still hungry for other things, young enough to start a new life, and well before I became a permanent, fossilized part of the system—I refused to become one of the poor, glassy-eyed creatures that wander the hallways at HQS.

And when I left, I realized something else: I'd spent most of my life searching for legitimacy, for the acceptance inherent in belonging to an elite group. More than anything, I wanted that identity and purpose and comradery.

But as I've reached the middle of my life, I understand more and more that such a quest has largely been pointless. While the CIA provided an incredible existence, the cadre I so desperately wanted to join wasn't worth the struggle. This is partly because such a group has no legitimate members—maybe no large organization comprised of strangers does. And it's partly because it's far more important that I be the one to accept myself.

Maybe that's the grandest (and most ironic) lesson the Agency taught me.

In short, I am immensely grateful to have been part of such an organization. It offered me an extraordinary life.

Like any relationship, I look back occasionally and remember the good times. Half of me would love to be with her again. Meanwhile, my other half doesn't miss her, celebrates that the relationship is over, and would be happy to never set eyes on her again—especially these days since she's really let herself go.

So I return to who I am. I look to myself and love my life, like everyone should.

And that's all you really need to know.

Class dismissed.

Acknowledgments

I thank my parents for raising me the right way, the Agency for giving me a great career, and a few colleagues for sharing their friendship and comradery. I also thank my editor Meghan Voss and book designer Michelle Argyle for their superb assistance.

About the Author

A CIA Case Officer for twenty years, Professor Millick served in a dozen countries, saw wars and revolutions, and worked on the front lines of history. This is his first book about the Agency.

Made in the USA
Middletown, DE
29 November 2021

53760325R00111